BIG
DATA
SMALL DEVICES

INVESTIGATING THE
NATURAL WORLD
········· USING ·········
REAL-TIME DATA

BIG DATA

SMALL DEVICES

INVESTIGATING THE
NATURAL WORLD
········ USING ········
REAL-TIME DATA

Donna Governor
Michael Bowen
Eric Brunsell

National Science Teachers Association

Arlington, Virginia

National Science Teachers Association

Claire Reinburg, Director
Wendy Rubin, Managing Editor
Rachel Ledbetter, Associate Editor
Amanda Van Beuren, Associate Editor
Donna Yudkin, Book Acquisitions Coordinator

ART AND DESIGN
Will Thomas Jr., Director
Himabindu Bichali, Graphic Designer, cover and
    interior design

PRINTING AND PRODUCTION
Catherine Lorrain, Director

NATIONAL SCIENCE TEACHERS ASSOCIATION
David L. Evans, Executive Director
David Beacom, Publisher

1840 Wilson Blvd., Arlington, VA 22201
www.nsta.org/store
For customer service inquiries, please call 800-277-5300.

NSTA is committed to publishing material that promotes the best in inquiry-based science education. However, conditions of actual use may vary, and the safety procedures and practices described in this book are intended to serve only as a guide. Additional precautionary measures may be required. NSTA and the authors do not warrant or represent that the procedures and practices in this book meet any safety code or standard of federal, state, or local regulations. NSTA and the authors disclaim any liability for personal injury or damage to property arising out of or relating to the use of this book, including any of the recommendations, instructions, or materials contained therein.

PERMISSIONS
Book purchasers may photocopy, print, or e-mail up to five copies of an NSTA book chapter for personal use only; this does not include display or promotional use. Elementary, middle, and high school teachers may reproduce forms, sample documents, and single NSTA book chapters needed for classroom or noncommercial, professional-development use only. E-book buyers may download files to multiple personal devices but are prohibited from posting the files to third-party servers or websites, or from passing files to non-buyers. For additional permission to photocopy or use material electronically from this NSTA Press book, please contact the Copyright Clearance Center (CCC) (*www.copyright.com*; 978-750-8400). Please access *www.nsta.org/permissions* for further information about NSTA's rights and permissions policies.

Library of Congress Cataloging-in-Publication Data
Names: Governor, Donna, 1957- | Bowen, Michael, 1962- | Brunsell, Eric.
Title: Big data, small devices : investigating the natural world using real-time data / Donna Governor, Michael Bowen, Eric Brunsell.
Description: Arlington, VA : National Science Teachers Association, [2017] | Includes bibliographical references and index.
Identifiers: LCCN 2016057882 | ISBN 9781681402765 (print)
Subjects: LCSH: Earth sciences--Computer-assisted instruction | Environmental sciences--Computer-assisted instruction. | Computer-assisted instruction.
Classification: LCC QE26.3 .G68 2017 | DDC 550.78/5--dc23 LC record available at *https://lccn.loc.gov/2016057882*

e-ISBN: 978-1-68140-277-2

Contents

PART 1: USING REAL-TIME DATA IN THE CLASSROOM

PAGE 3

1

WHAT ARE REAL-TIME DATA?

5

3

CONDUCTING INVESTIGATIONS WITH REAL-TIME DATA

27

2

TECHNOLOGY TIPS AND TRICKS

17

4

DATA TYPES, REPRESENTATION, AND ANALYSIS

43

PART 2: SAMPLE ACTIVITIES USING REAL-TIME DATA
PAGE 65

5

INVESTIGATIONS USING REAL-TIME ATMOSPHERE DATA
71

7

INVESTIGATIONS USING REAL-TIME GEOSPHERE DATA
141

6

INVESTIGATIONS USING REAL-TIME BIOSPHERE DATA
111

8

INVESTIGATIONS USING REAL-TIME HYDROSPHERE DATA
171

INVESTIGATIONS USING REAL-TIME CELESTIAL SPHERE DATA

201

PART 3: GOING FURTHER

PAGE 229

BEYOND THE DATA

231

REAL-TIME CITIZEN SCIENCE

239

ABOUT THE AUTHORS

Donna Governor is an assistant professor of science education at the University of North Georgia (UNG). Before joining UNG in the fall of 2016, she was a high school Earth and advanced placement environmental science teacher in Cumming, Georgia. She has taught all grade levels as a K–12 classroom teacher for more than 30 years. Donna holds a PhD in Science Education from the University of Georgia and has won multiple awards, including the Presidential Award for Excellence in Science Teaching (2007) and the Outstanding Earth Science Teacher for Georgia (2014). Donna is a past president of the Georgia Science Teachers Association and has served as a district director for the National Science Teachers Association (NSTA). She also has been a presenter at local, state, and national conferences for more than 20 years.

Michael Bowen holds a doctorate from the University of Victoria in Canada. After studying the research practices of field biologists, he developed curricula for middle school students that were tested with sixth- and seventh-grade students in the classroom and outdoors. Following a postdoctoral fellowship in the sociology department at Trent University in Ontario, he became a member of the faculties of education at three Canadian universities: Lakehead University, the University of New Brunswick, and Mount Saint Vincent University (where he is now an associate professor). His research has been presented at national and international conferences in Canada, Europe, and the United States. Michael has served as a district director for NSTA and has co-authored two other books for NSTA Press and numerous articles for its journals.

Eric Brunsell is an associate professor of science education in the Department of Teaching and Learning and the director of the professional education programs at the University of Wisconsin Oshkosh in Oshkosh, Wisconsin. Eric earned his EdD in curriculum and instruction with an emphasis in science education from Montana State University. He is a former high school science teacher and has served as NSTA district 12 director and on the NSTA Board of Directors as the professional development division director. He is also the chief operations officer for the Wisconsin Society of Science Teachers. Eric has written two other books, edited two book compilations, and provided professional development sessions and presentations throughout the United States and internationally.

ACKNOWLEDGMENTS

Donna would like to acknowledge Dr. Tim Slater for introducing her to the world of real-time data when the internet was still new. Dr. Slater has been an important mentor to Donna over the years and given her multiple opportunities to grow and develop as an education professional.

Mike's interest in real-world "messy" data and how that could be represented in complex graphs heightened during his MSc(Res) with encouragement from his supervisor, John Sprague. During his work as a middle school science teacher, his eighth-grade students inspired him further in this area, and his PhD supervisor, Wolff-Michael Roth, was a wonderful mentor and supported his later research and writing about graphing, data table use, and other data literacy areas.

Eric would like to acknowledge David Braunschweig for showing him the power of having students use data to create and revise models of scientific phenomena. Eric was a student teacher with David in his Madison, Wisconsin, physics classroom 20 years ago.

PREFACE

In the HBO (Home Box Office) series *From the Earth to the Moon*, there is a dramatization of the field geology training that was provided to the Apollo astronauts assigned to the final three missions. Geologist Lee Silver (played by David Clennon) offered an analogy about "context." He said, "If you brought me a dead cat, I can tell you two things about it: It was a cat, and it is dead. If you told me you found it in the middle of the road … what killed the cat? What if you found it in the kitchen of your favorite restaurant?" He was referring to context as the difference between road kill and a meal.

And what does access to large data sets provide to students? It provides a number of supports for learning—most importantly, context. As has been frequently cited in science education reform documents, science learning has often been approached in a manner that has been very broad at the expense of depth. Coverage, it seems, can be the enemy of understanding (Gardner 1991). Context can provide the necessary depth for understanding by making explicit the connections between the science content that we wish for students to learn and the real world. The real world is complex and defies simple understandings— or rather, simple understandings are inadequate for grasping the complex, multivariate patterns that are inherent to the natural world.

This volume embraces the fact that the natural world is complex and multivariate, but through the three-dimensional learning structure of *A Framework for K–12 Science Education* (*Framework;* NRC 2012), this complexity is not necessarily complicated. Complex systems operate on a variety of scales and evolve over time with the amount of energy present in the system (Fichter, Pyle, and Whitmeyer 2010). Understanding systems, a fundamental part of the crosscutting concepts, does not mean that a deterministic outcome is available. Rather, recognizable patterns can be displayed by comparing data related to natural Earth phenomena, whether they are the mapped distribution of earthquake epicenters or the variations in temperature and humidity with altitude across locations. The more data that are available, the more robust are the inferences that can be made regarding complex relationships, and the clearer is the pattern that can emerge. By analyzing changes in the patterns, other crosscutting concepts can be accessed, such as stability and change; cause and effect: mechanism and explanation; and scale, proportion, and quantity.

The other critical aspect of the *Framework* that goes beyond the disciplinary core ideas is the practices employed by scientists and engineers as they go about their work. This volume is well-positioned to use the science and engineering practices to provide context as well. As was illustrated in the now infamous "climategate" email hacking incident (Cook 2016), the public has a different understanding of "data manipulation" than scientists employ. To properly analyze and interpret data, particularly large data sets, scientists have to organize the data in a manner that makes sense for generating and testing models, as well as for generating arguments from these data. A connective practice is the use of mathematical and computational thinking, which not only provides context to scientific thinking, but also provides a platform for teachers of mathematics and science to reconcile language and terminology differences that cause students to have endless frustration.

Context for large data sets thus is critical not only to scientific understanding, but also to learning how to understand the natural world from a scientific standpoint. Fundamentally woven in the performance expectations within the *Next Generation Science Standards* (*NGSS*; NGSS Lead States 2013), context is the basis by which we can distinguish ourselves from the automated devices we use to collect such data and evaluate whether or not the data are accurate, valuable, and sufficient. I trust you will find this volume useful not just in teaching science, but also in using science as a way to grasp the complexity of the natural world with awe and wonder, instead of fear.

Eric J. Pyle, PhD

NSTA Division Director, Preservice Teacher Preparation

Professor, Department of Geology and Environmental Science

Coordinator, Science Teacher Preparation, College of Science and Mathematics

James Madison University

REFERENCES

Cook, J. 2016. What do the 'Climategate' hacked CRU emails tell us? Skeptical Science. *www.skepticalscience.com/Climategate-CRU-emails-hacked.htm.*

Fichter, L. S., E. J. Pyle, and S. J. Whitmeyer. 2010. Strategies and rubrics for teaching chaos and complex systems theories as elaborating, self-organizing, and fractionating evolutionary systems. *Journal of Geoscience Education* 58 (2): 65–85.

Gardner, H. 1991. *The unschooled mind: How children think and how schools should teach.* New York: Basic Books.

National Research Council (NRC) 2012. *A framework for K–12 science education: Practices, crosscutting concepts, and core ideas.* Washington, DC: National Academies Press.

NGSS Lead States. 2013. *Next Generation Science Standards: For states, by states.* Washington, DC: National Academies Press. *www.nextgenscience.org/next-generation-science-standards.*

INTRODUCTION

Smartphones and tablets are now in the hands of even our youngest learners. As teachers, we are encouraged to use bring-your-own-technology (BYOT), but often are not sure how to transform smartphones and tablets into a valuable learning tool for meaningful instruction.

One answer lies in using a number of free smartphone and tablet apps that provide "real-time" data to explore Earth and environmental science concepts. These are data collected and made available in real time, or nearly so. Real-time data can be found on websites such as the U.S. Geological Survey (USGS), the National Oceanic and Atmospheric Administration (NOAA), the U.S. Environmental Protection Agency (EPA), NASA, and the National Weather Service (NWS). These are all government agencies that provide free data products such as weather and earthquake information, streamflow data, toxic waste information, times of celestial events, and planetary data. These data are free, and a multitude of apps have been developed that access and visualize them, in most cases at no cost. Students can access this information on websites; however, allowing students to investigate concepts using their smartphones in app-based activities allows them to be more engaged in science investigations and teaches them how to turn the technology they carry with them all the time into a useful learning tool.

Using real data in classroom investigations aligns with the following *Next Generation Science Standards* (*NGSS*) science and engineering practices:

- Asking questions and defining problems

- Planning and carrying out investigations

- Analyzing and interpreting data

- Developing and using models

- Constructing explanations and designing solutions

- Engaging in argument from evidence

- Using mathematics and computational thinking

- Obtaining, evaluating, and communicating information

The *NGSS* crosscutting concepts involved in real-time data investigations include the following:

- Patterns

- Cause and effect: Mechanism and explanation

- Scale, proportion, and quantity

- Systems and system models

- Energy and matter: Flows, cycles, and conservation

- Structure and function

- Stability and change

This book is designed to help the classroom Earth and environmental science teacher develop student investigations that use real-time data. It includes information on the technology and classroom implementation aspects of accessing and using data for meaningful learning. Sample lesson plans are included that showcase specific data and the apps that include them. But more importantly, this book provides the classroom teacher with a set of tools to develop investigations with any online-accessible data. Finally, exploring real-time data is not limited to independent experiences—collecting and sharing data with others can promote collaborative scientific investigations. With the use of multiple web-based applications and apps for personal devices, opportunities exist for everyone to participate in citizen science programs.

PART 1

USING REAL-TIME DATA IN THE CLASSROOM

WHAT ARE REAL-TIME DATA?

Every time an earthquake happens anywhere on our planet, the U.S. Geological Survey (USGS) records its location, magnitude, and depth. This information is available immediately through the USGS website. Most people are familiar with the data provided by the National Weather Service. Through its website, information about surface and atmospheric conditions such as barometric pressure, wind speed, wind direction, and humidity are updated hourly and available in real time.

The National Data Buoy Center (NDBC), a division of the National Oceanic and Atmospheric Administration (NOAA), provides data from hundreds of buoys in every ocean and other major body of water in the world (Figure 1.1), including latitude, longitude, wind speed, wave height, air temperature, water temperature, and wave period. These data are updated hourly for most stations and posted online in real time. As conditions change, data are updated and made immediately accessible to anyone, anywhere.

Figure 1.1. Example of NDBC buoy data

Source: National Data Buoy Center, *www.ndbc.noaa.gov.*

Other data collected by various government agencies and distributed via the web in real time include stream quality, groundwater levels, toxic waste amounts, ozone levels, tide tables, Moon phase, and sunrise and sunset times. Because these data are provided by various government agencies, they are free of cost and available for use by any individual or organization. Their availability is a public service that is widely used by scientists all over the world.

These real-time data provide a record of the heartbeat and pulse of our planet and are a rich source of information, perfect for student investigations into how Earth's systems work. Data accessed in real time helps students connect the events in their lives to the world of science. Data sets can be fully explored by anyone with access for investigating patterns and relationships. Long-term trends can be analyzed using data collected over time. Alternatively, data from multiple sources can be compared to identify variables that interact and affect each other.

ACCESSING REAL-TIME DATA FOR STUDENT INVESTIGATIONS

Through a series of fortunate events, Donna was asked in 1995 to be a part of team to develop an internet-based curriculum with real-time data using a new technology interface called the internet. Web browsers were relatively new at that time, replacing proprietary services such as Prodigy, Compuserve, and America Online (AOL). Online modems had advanced to what seemed like incredible speeds and a brand new world of information was at our fingertips. She was thrilled to be asked to participate in this project and upgraded to an Apple Macintosh 500 series computer. With 5 megabytes (MB) of memory, 100 MB of hard drive space, and a processing speed of 33 MHz, it connected at lightning speeds of 56 kbit/s with a brand new modem.

This new type of technology interface was amazing and opened up a world of information with instant access. Not only could teachers communicate in real-time, but they also could also access data collected by scientists from all over the world. The uniqueness of the internet as a teaching tool was not in any single feature, but rather in its richness and diversity of resources and capabilities. Text, graphics, audio, video, animations, communications, and interactivity were all included in the web environment. For the first time, teachers could bring real-world problems and investigations into their classrooms. Time and place no longer limited educational opportunities, and Donna was pleased to be a participant in these early online communities.

One of the first real-time data investigations Donna did with her students involved tracking earthquake activity for a 30-day period. At the time, she was teaching a multi-age class of fourth and fifth graders using an interdisciplinary approach. Each morning, she would have a different pair of students connect to the USGS website and find out where earthquakes had occurred during the previous 24 hours. As a class, the students would use latitude and longitude to find the earthquakes' epicenters on a large map on a bulletin board, and then mark those locations with pushpins that were color-coded by magnitude.

By the end of the month, students could clearly see the outline of the major tectonic plates and where the higher-magnitude earthquakes occurred. Donna's students read about earthquakes, both fiction and non-fiction. Over the course of the unit, she watched her students engage in an integrated and authentic learning experience using real-time data. And she was hooked. The internet and the rich sources of data that could be accessed online had the potential to change the way science was taught.

Similarly, Eric used online archived weather data with middle school students to develop an understanding of climate. Students used data from a fifteen-year period to identify temperature and rainfall patterns in multiple cities. They used these patterns to predict future weather and to identify different climate zones in the United States.

Over the past 20 years, technology has taken us on a wild ride. What seemed like lightning speed in 1995 would frustrate an online community user beyond belief today. The amount of data available has increased exponentially. Real-time investigations have continued to be a part of teaching science; however, two major changes have occurred that have advanced how we present and use real-time data. One is in data's accessibility; the other is in the users themselves.

Smartphones and tablets are relatively new technologies are changing the way we live and interact with the world. Not only are we connected for voice, but we also have a world of data at our fingertips wherever we are. Also, although not every student has a personal technology device, it is becoming more common than not for students to walk into our classrooms internet-connected via one (usually plugged in through earbuds). A few years ago, whatever data Donna and Eric wanted to use for student investigations could be accessed in real-time, but because there were few computers and limited connectivity in the classroom, it was difficult to manage. Teachers had to either project the data that they wanted students to interact with on a whiteboard or screen or provide paper copies of them. Now, enough students have smartphones that a teacher need only provide students with a uniform resource locator (URL) or a device app, and they can gather their own data individually or in small groups.

Not only has the internet revolutionized how we teach, but smartphones have revolutionized how we access and use the internet. These devices are windows to a world of data that are reported in real time and ready for student investigation. Research done as early as 2001 with Palm-based handheld devices showed that "handheld-based probes augmented inquiry-based investigations with real-time data and visualizations, which in turn increased the students' engagement and let them concentrate on science rather than logistics" (Tatar et al. 2003, p. 31).

The second major change that has affected how we teach is in the nature of the students. Students, as well as an ever-increasing population of teachers, are part of the digital generation. Born after 1990, digital natives have grown up with technology substantially influencing every aspect of their lives. They are so dependent on their smartphones that it often is difficult for teachers to separate them from their devices during instruction! But today's students use technology not just to chat and socialize, but also to solve everyday problems. Our students use their devices to take pictures of homework assignments on the whiteboard, set reminders for assignments in their calendars, and set up virtual study groups for tests. Today's students see technology as an integral part of their world and find technology solutions for almost every need. The use of smartphones and tablets to access real-time data might not be something today's students would do on their own, but would be an application that they might expect. For teachers, finding and accessing the right data and determining the best approach to using them are often challenging.

Data are provided by federal agencies such as NASA, USGS, NOAA, and the Environmental Protection Agency (EPA). Other data are collected and shared online by universities and private organizations; some sites are funded by National Science Foundation (NSF) grants, and others, by nonprofit organizations. Regardless of the source, there is an abundance of real-time data out there.

Our focus for this book is on using real-time data for Earth and environmental science. We have organized and presented such resources by sphere in chapters five through nine. The atmosphere chapter includes information related to the weather, climate, air pollution, and more. The world of living organisms and how they interact with their environment are part of the biosphere chapter. Data on earthquakes, landfills, and soils are grouped in the geosphere chapter. The hydrosphere chapter covers ocean currents, sea-surface temperature, streamflow, water pollution, and water quality. Glaciers, snow pack and ice caps are part of the cryosphere, but for purposes of this book are in the hydrosphere chapter. Finally, we cover phenomena such as seasonal changes and phases of the Moon in the chapter on the celestial sphere.

USING CROSSCUTTING CONCEPTS WITH REAL-TIME DATA

Regardless of its source, how scientists use data is reasonably consistent across all disciplines. Common themes, or crosscutting concepts, are basic to developing student understanding of the work scientists do. These themes provide "an organization framework for connecting knowledge" (NRC 2012). When real-time data are used in classroom investigations, students build on these fundamental concepts. The crosscutting concepts facilitated by the use of real-time data include the following:

- Patterns

- Cause and effect: Mechanism and explanation

- Scale, proportion, and quantity

- Systems and system models

- Energy and matter: Flows, cycles, and conservation

- Structure and function

- Stability and change

In addition to providing an organizing framework for scientific knowledge, the cross-cutting concepts defined in the *NGSS* provide a lens through which scientists (and our students) can view new scientific phenomena. Describing a system being observed, identifying patterns, and looking for changes in data are good starting points for making sense of the world around us. In the classroom, it is often easier to organize crosscutting concepts into four of those categories that are closely related: Patterns, Cause and Effect, Systems and System Models, and Stability and Change. When analyzing phenomena, encourage your students to start by asking the questions in Table 1.1. The remainder of this chapter provides examples of some of these crosscutting concepts in use.

Table 1.1. Data analysis questions based on the *NGSS* crosscutting concepts

Systems	Stability and Change
Questions • What is the system? • What is happening in the system? • How are the parts of the system related? • How do energy and matter flow in the system? **Crosscutting concepts** • Systems and system models • Energy and matter: Flows, cycles, and conservation	**Questions** • Does the system change? How quickly does it change? • What scale (for example, microscopic, macroscopic) should I be thinking about? • Does the amount of "stuff" matter? **Crosscutting concepts** • Stability and change • Scale, proportion, and quantity
Cause and Effect	**Patterns**
Questions • What might be causing the effects that I see? • Is the structure related to the function? **Crosscutting concepts** • Cause and effect: Mechanism and explanation • Structure and function	**Questions** • What patterns do I notice? • How are those patterns related to others that I have seen? **Crosscutting concept** • Patterns

PATTERNS

Patterns are evident in the world around us and are often recognizable in the data scientists collect. Scientists identify patterns to build explanations for how the world works and to predict events. Patterns that are evident in data can inspire questions that build an understanding of natural phenomena. Explanations can arise from the correspondences in the patterns, but also sometimes from the variations in the patterns or even the absence of a pattern.

For example, consider the data shown in Table 1.2, which were collected by the National Weather Service on May 10–11, 2015, and accessed in real time. Although we could have pulled data for many different variables, we chose to concentrate on wind speed, wind direction, and air pressure. In addition, Figure 1.2 shows how winds circulate around low-pressure systems. What patterns are evident in the data? Is the pressure increasing or decreasing? What about the wind speed? The air pressure? Are there any apparent correlations?

Figure 1.2. Winds around a low-pressure system

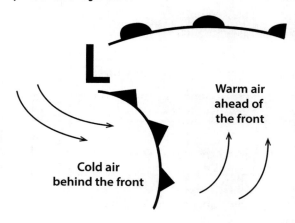

Cold air behind the front

Warm air ahead of the front

Correlating wind speed and air pressure does not seem to show an identifiable pattern. Over time, air pressure falls and then begins to rise again. When you look carefully at the data, the one pattern that emerges is the relationship between air pressure and wind direction. Right before air pressure reaches its lowest point, the winds are from the southeast. When the weather system has passed and the air pressure has begun to rise, the winds shift and are from the west. By identifying this simple pattern, students can build an explanation for how weather systems work. To build an understanding of natural phenomena, data can be collected from multiple events in real time to see whether this pattern is consistent and repeatable.

CAUSE AND EFFECT: MECHANISM AND EXPLANATION

Questions can be used to guide students in establishing causal relationships as they work with patterns. In exploring and mapping earthquake data from a period of time, students easily see that whereas earthquakes can happen anywhere, they often occur in the Pacific Ocean in what is referred to as the Pacific Ring of Fire (Figure 1.3). This tectonic ring is located along tectonic plate boundaries where the Pacific Plate is subducting under other plates.

As students explore earthquake patterns using real-time data, they can see that there is a cause-and-effect relationship between earthquakes and plate boundaries. They can identify the forces at work and the hazards associated with plate boundaries, and can use this relationship to help understand natural events in the world and the evidence scientists use in developing theories.

Table 1.2. Weather data for Des Moines, Iowa, from 7:00 p.m. on May 10, 2015, through 7:00 a.m. on May 11, 2015

Time	Wind Direction	Wind Speed (Knots)	Air Pressure (Millibars)
7 p.m.	S	12	1,008.0
8 p.m.	SE	10	1,007.6
9 p.m.	SE	10	1,007.7
10 p.m.	SE	14	1,007.6
11 p.m.	Calm	0	1,007.3
Midnight	SW	15	1,007.8
1 a.m.	W	18	1,008.3
2 a.m.	W	13	1,008.9
3 a.m.	W	12	1,008.7
4 a.m.	W	20	1,009.0
5 a.m.	W	12	1,009.6
6 a.m.	W	13	1,009.3
7 a.m.	W	17	1,010.0

Data source: National Weather Service. *www.weather.gov.*

Figure 1.3. Pacific Ring of Fire

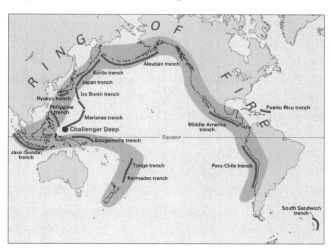

Source: U.S. Geological Survey. *http://pubs.usgs.gov/gip/dynamic/fire.html.*

SYSTEMS AND SYSTEM MODELS

The best way for students to explore Earth and environmental science is through a systems approach. In science, systems are related factors that interact to form a single unit. In Earth and environmental science, these are usually categorized as the geosphere, atmosphere, hydrosphere, and biosphere. These systems are bounded by physical criteria and forces, but they interact and affect each other in complex ways. Exploring real-time data can help students build conceptual models to form an understanding of the interactions within and among systems. Graphs are often helpful in visualizing data and useful for students for constructing models.

The NDBC data in Table 1.3 are a good example of how real-time data can be used to help students build conceptual models to better understand systems and their interactions. Surface waves in the ocean are caused by wind, with speed, duration, and fetch (distance) all affecting wave height. The data show a correlation between wind speed and wave height (Figure 1.4). Interactions between the atmosphere and the hydrosphere are evident, as students conclude that, in general, the greater the wind speed, the higher the waves; however, it is clear from the outliers present that something other than wind speed is affecting wave height. Wind duration and fetch are not in the available data, but provide a good explanation for the outlying data.

When the data are appropriate for scatterplot analysis, a trend line can show a mathematical correlation between variables. This serves as a mathematical model that is valuable for predicting how a system will respond to future interactions. In the example discussed above, the slope is 0.39 with a correlation coefficient of 87% (indicating that most of the values are very close to the line of best fit and that it is a strong correlation). Using real-time data to investigate components of any system will help students build conceptual models and develop a greater understanding of the science.

STABILITY AND CHANGE

Understanding stability and change in Earth's systems and the environment is important for understanding how nature works. Systems are stable in that the flows of energy and matter are steady and predictable. Although they are not considered static, Earth's systems are in dynamic equilibrium and its patterns vary in rhythmic and cyclic ways. Tides rise and fall with the phases of the Moon, increased precipitation affects streamflow, and increased altitude at a given latitude results in decreased temperatures. Over time these patterns seem unchanging; however, they can be destabilized when balances in matter and energy within a system are disrupted. Real-time data are useful in helping students to identify natural cycles and explore forces of change within and across Earth's systems.

An example of data comes from exploring high and low temperatures on a given date. During the 45-year period from 1970 to 2015, the mean (average) high temperature on

Table 1.3. NDBC data for wind speed and wave height

Buoy	Wind Speed (Knots)	Wave Height (Feet)
44014	23.3	7.2
44025	5.8	2.6
41040	17.5	7.5
41043	15.5	6.9
42058	25.3	11.5
42002	15.5	6.2
42039	7.8	2.3
42001	13.6	4.3
42300	20.0	7.9
41010	11.7	4.6
41048	9.7	3.6
44008	5.8	3.3

Data source: National Data Buoy Center, *www.ndbc.noaa.gov.*

Figure 1.4. Scatterplot analysis of the data in Table 1.3

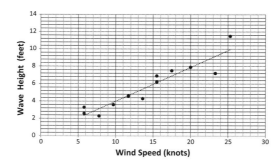

The trend line shows a mathematical correlation between wind speed and wave height.

Table 1.4. High and low temperatures for Atlanta, Georgia, measured biennially on May 11 from 1984 to 2014

Year	Low (°F)	High (°F)
1984	46	79
1986	59	79
1988	55	79
1990	46	72
1992	54	84
1994	59	82
1996	64	88
1998	59	75
2000	57	88
2002	63	84
2004	63	82
2006	61	70
2008	63	81
2010	52	79
2012	54	79
2014	63	84

Data source: Weather History Explorer app.

May 11 in Atlanta, Georgia, was 80°F and the mean low was 57°F. Table 1.4 shows the high and low temperatures in degrees Fahrenheit, measured biennially on this date from 1984 to 2014. Data for the 1984–2014 period show a relatively stable pattern, with a narrow range of temperatures such as can be expected on a spring day in the southeastern United States, based on the data for the period (Figure 1.5).

Looking at variations from real-time data can help students understand how different factors can create change. On May 11, 2015, this station recorded a high temperature of 90°F and a low of 66°F. Although well above the normal high and low for that date, these temperatures are within a range of conditions under which scientists would expect to find in a stable system. Questions that arise from such an investigation will help students understand not only the system, but also the conditions that might bring about change.

Figure 1.5. High and low temperatures for Atlanta, Georgia, measured on May 11 biennially from 1984 to 2014

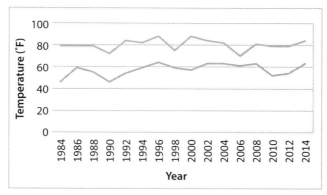

Data source: Weather History Explorer app.

SUMMARY

Using real-time data is one of the best ways to get students to explore the natural world. The data inherently allow students to better understand the themes of doing science as they participate in meaningful investigations. Events they observe happening in the world around them can be quantified and explored by identifying patterns, hypothesizing about cause and effect, developing models of system dynamics, and identifying indicators of stability and change. Unlike earlier generations of students, students today have a world of big data available to them at any given moment on small devices they carry with them at all times. The data are limitless, relevant to their daily lives, current, and accessible in real time. Now, let's find out how to access that world of data!

REFERENCES

National Data Buoy Center. *www.ndbc.noaa.gov.*

National Research Council (NRC). 2012. *A framework for K–12 science education: Practices, crosscutting concepts, and core ideas.* Washington, DC: National Academies Press.

National Weather Service. *www.weather.gov.*

Savchenko, V. 2014. *Weather History Explorer* app. Sofia, Bulgaria.

Tatar, D., J. Roschelle, P. Vahey, and W. R. Penuel. 2003. Handhelds go to school: Lessons learned. *IEEE Computer* 36 (9): 30–37.

U.S. Geological Survey (USGS). Ring of Fire plate tectonic map. *http://pubs.usgs.gov/gip/dynamic/fire.html.*

TECHNOLOGY TIPS AND TRICKS

There are many options for accessing real-time data. Desktops, laptops, tablets, and smartphones can all be used to access the data your students need to participate in real-time data investigations. Some students will be on Windows-based computers and Android devices; others will be on iPhones or iPads or using a Mac operating system. For the teacher who wants students to access data, it helps to know a little about these different options and how to navigate some of the issues students will encounter as they turn their devices into tools to conduct their investigations. In this chapter, we will look at some of the basics you need to know to access and use technology for retrieving and processing data in student investigations.

ACCESSING YOUR SCHOOL'S NETWORK

The most important consideration in using internet-based data is how to access it; school district technology departments have rules and regulations governing how technology may be accessed and used. Most school districts have policies in place that maximize access to internet-based resources but also protect students from inappropriate content. The guidelines for school districts set by the Children's Internet Protection Act (CIPA) are incorporated into each district's Acceptable Use Policies (AUPs). Such policies incorporate a variety of tools and rules to help keep students from accessing material that is inappropriate or potentially harmful. Filters, monitors, and blocking software are the most common way for districts to comply with CIPA, but the implementation of CIPA is different in every school system (Bosco 2013). Some systems block all videos, chat functions, and social networking sites, some search engines, and some website domain extensions (for example, they may allow access to .edu and .gov websites but not to .net or .biz sites). Many systems also log student use of different websites so that should a problem arise, a technology administrator can access a student's (or teacher's) browsing history. In our experience, districts do not ban government (*.gov*) or education websites (*.edu*), which is one reason that the online resources for data we have shared in this book are primarily government resources (for example, U.S. Geological Survey [USGS], National Oceanic and Atmospheric Administration [NOAA], and Environmental Protection Agency [EPA]). And policies do evolve. Access to YouTube at one time was blocked in Donna's school district (and in others), but now is allowed with the activation of YouTube's "Safety Mode."

Teachers should be aware of their district's policies before planning a student investigation using real-time data, and verify that students will indeed be able to access the information. Some districts maintain a list of blocked words that students cannot use in search-engine searches and that filter the search results that will display. Such limitations are in place for student protection; however, sometimes they interfere with legitimate learning activities. For instance, a school's information technology filters can get in the way of accessing websites that include inappropriate terms used in a totally appropriate context. To deal with problems such as this, most school districts have a procedure for granting access to blocked websites, so it is best to make sure websites referred to in this book work with your district's filters before incorporating them into students' investigations. Some districts allow students and teachers different levels of access, so you should verify that each website is available for students, even if works with a teacher account.

School systems are increasingly opting for bring-your-own-technology (BYOT) access, which allows students to bring laptops, tablets, and smartphones from home. Students who connect personal devices to the school network also will be limited by the district's AUP, and often are required to acknowledge in writing that they will use BYOT access in accordance with district policies. District policies that were established on the basis of CIPA requirements often are inadequate. Keep in mind that CIPA was enacted in 2001, long before smartphones, social media, hot spots, and data plans. Many districts are struggling with how to balance their responsibility under the law with the realities of today's technology. Some districts are moving to a "Responsible Use Policy" that shifts some of the accountability to students in an effort to accommodate BYOT while recognizing filtering limitations.

Students accessing websites and apps through their data plans are not subject to the same oversight and limitations as those accessing through the network. This can be a mixed blessing and should be approached with caution. For example, some districts do not allow students to download apps over their network. So, if you want to use apps to access real-time data, students might need to have to use their own data plan to download the app in class. This can be a problem for students with limited data plans. Networks that block all app downloads cannot single out one app for an exception as easily as they can for web addresses. So, you might want to ask students to download the apps they will need at home. Donna has found that if she tells students they can only have their phones out if the desired app is installed, students will suddenly find free space on their phones and available data on their plan!

OPERATING SYSTEMS

One of the most obvious issues with technology use in school concerns the type of operating system that runs computers and devices. Most school systems choose a platform and implement it district-wide, with labs and laptop carts using the same type of operating system. There are advantages and disadvantages to each, and whether your district uses a

Mac or Windows system really is not a challenge. However, students might bring in their own technology, which can be different from what the teacher is used to. This does not usually present a problem on computers because data are accessed through web browsers, which are nearly identical in function regardless of platform. If your student brings in a laptop with a different operating system, he or she will probably be able to navigate data websites easily without help.

Most tablets and smartphones use either an Apple (iOS) or an Android operating system. There are a few Windows-based tablets and smartphones, but these are less common (although they are becoming more affordable). Between tablets and smartphones, there are more differences in how data are accessed because of the differences in web browsers and apps used for each type of system. These can be more challenging to manage when collecting real-time data, but can be easily used if you know what to expect. Although some apps that allow students access to real-time data are available on both platforms, many are only available on one platform or the other. Many apps are developed by individuals or small software firms who might not be able to justify the expense and complexity of writing native apps for more than one operating system. Even if the data are not accessible through an app on a particular device, they are often accessible through an internet browser.

RESPONSIVE DESIGN

One of the more common approaches for organizations that want to provide data on small devices is to build websites with responsive design techniques, which run exclusively in a browser but can scale content to fit large, medium, or small devices. For example, if you are viewing a responsive web page on a desktop computer, you would see the full website page; however, on a tablet or a smartphone, that website's content would compress and "snap" to the size of that smaller screen. Responsive software makes choices about what content is shown and which becomes hidden, based on the device type and size.

One way to tell whether a website uses responsive design is by opening it on a desktop or laptop computer and reducing the size of the browser window. If the content adapts intelligently to the window size—collapses menus and reorganizes itself—the site has been built using responsive design and will work as a web-based app on a smartphone or tablet. However, if all you see in the smaller browser window is a fraction of the original content, then the design is not responsive. The USGS *Earthquake* webpage for the latest events has a responsive design (Figure 2.1, p. 20). A full-screen version on your computer shows data for recent earthquakes and a map; however, with a smaller window or on a smartphone screen, you will see just the data and must select a separate icon to view the map.

Using responsive design websites in lieu of native apps has advantages and disadvantages. One advantage is that students can access the data through the browser on a tablet or smartphone without needing to download an app. Also, the controls and settings are integrated into the browser, making it easier to navigate. However, this type of data access

Figure 2.1. Screenshot of the USGS *Earthquake* website on a laptop screen (left) and a smartphone (right), showing how websites designed to be responsive adapt to the screen size of the device being used

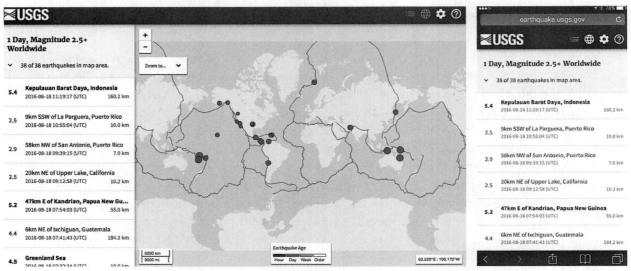

Source: U.S. Geological Survey. *http://earthquake.usgs.gov/earthquakes/map.*

does not work well with highly interactive uses. It also is not as fast or as customizable as a native app, and might not allow use of special device features built into portable devices, such as an accelerometer or a camera. Sometimes only certain pages on a website are built with responsive design, so be sure to provide students with specific pages to view when gathering real-time data from their browser.

NATIVE APPS

Native apps are developed for specific devices that use a single operating system. To develop the same app for both an Android device and an iPhone, the app developer usually must write it twice—once in each language. Some developers use software with an integration platform designed to develop apps that run on both iOS and Android with a near-native look and feel. Sometimes such apps are not as good as those written in a native language, and they might not work well for highly interactive applications; however, in most cases, you will notice little difference. Regardless, many apps are only available for one platform or the other, so when you want to use apps for teaching, you should plan on using cross-platform apps, web-based apps, or native apps that are similar in the data they provide.

USING APPS FOR ACCESSING REAL-TIME DATA

Donna often prefers using apps over websites in her classroom when working with real-time data. She finds that many apps target specific data for student investigations, and students are confined to the data and resources provided in the app. This can help students focus and avoid distractions. The first requirement for any app is that it be free; you cannot expect students to pay for an app. Some apps are totally free, whereas for others, the free version has less functionality and a paid version has more functionality. With so many apps available for accessing real-time data, finding a free option usually is not a problem.

Figure 2.2.
Weather History Explorer **app icon**

Source: *Weather History Explorer* app.

The real challenge is finding the right app for each operating system. If you are really lucky, you will find an app that has been developed for both platforms. For example, one of the best apps for exploring climate is called *Weather History Explorer* (Figure 2.2), which is available for Android and iOS, with both versions having the same look and feel.

When looking through an app store online, availability of two identical app icons is a clue that an app might be available on both the iOS and Android platforms. Some organizations invest in building apps for both platforms. One example is the American Red Cross, whose excellent safety apps for natural disasters such as hurricanes, earthquakes, floods, and wildfires are available on both platforms. The United Nations also has identical apps for environmental science; for example, *FAO Now*, which deals with world hunger issues, and *Applifish*, which provides information about endangered marine species. It is worth the time to look for these apps before looking for apps for separate platforms.

Sometimes, the same app is not available for both operating system, and you have to find similar apps for each platform. This takes a little more effort. You can begin by searching for data apps within a web browser or an app store. Start with the device you have (iOS- or Android-based) and find an app you like. Identify its features you find most helpful, then look for a similar app for the other platform. It helps to have a student, colleague, or friend who can help with the search for

FINDING AN APP

There are several possible strategies for finding a usable app that you like:

- Browse the app selection in the "science" or "weather" section of the app store.
- Conduct an online search with terms such as "earthquake app" or "buoy app" – often the results returned will include someone's "top ten" list of apps for your desired data topic.
- Ask students to find apps dealing with your topic (for example, ocean currents, hurricanes, weather, earthquakes).

the alternative app and try it out on their device. Donna is an iPhone user and more than once has called her daughter to find an Android app that will provide the desired data. Alternatively, sometimes she just carefully evaluates the information and screenshots provided for each option in the app store to verify an app's suitability.

Today's students are digital natives and are likely to have far fewer problems than their teachers in interacting with apps. It often is unnecessary to spend a great deal of time figuring out all the nuances; just make sure the app will let you access the same data. For the lessons we provide in this book, we have recommended apps for each platform when a single, multiplatform app is not available. However, you might find an alternative app that you prefer.

Regardless of which apps you include in each lesson, you should check their settings and filters. The settings for many apps allow you to select the units you use. Science teachers usually want students to use metric units, such as kilometers for distance. For common use, most weather apps report air pressure in inches and temperature in Fahrenheit, but for real-time data investigations, students should work in millibars and degrees Celsius. Earthquake app settings generally default to report all events of magnitude 2.5 and higher; however, the number of earthquakes reported under that setting will be very high, and setting that filter to magnitude 4.0 or higher will return a manageable data set for students. On more than one occasion, Donna has asked her students with Android devices to help her find menu options.

You cannot always explore all aspects of your chosen parallel apps before a lesson, and sometimes problems arise when using an app for the first time. Students solve problems for each other so quickly that in most cases, such problems are resolved almost before you are even aware of them. (Having students work in groups can facilitate this.) Should a problem arise that cannot be solved, though, students will need to team up to gather data on one device or another, or will need to access data through a web browser. Donna usually ensures that each app-based lesson includes a universal resource locator (URL) for web-based data collection in case app problems arise or devices are unavailable.

USING QR CODES

A Quick Response Code (QR Code) is a two-dimensional, matrix bar code that uses an array of black and white squares that is encoded with a link to a website. Figure 2.3 is a QR Code that when scanned by a smartphone or tablet will take you directly to the home page of the National Science Teachers Association (NSTA). QR Codes are useful in investigations with real-time data because they can be generated to take students directly to websites or apps to download. Creating a QR Code is easy— just navigate to a QR Code–generating website and enter the URL of the desired web page. The matrix image produced can be added into your lesson, printed for handout, or projected onto the board. Students use a barcode scanner app to read the QR Code via their device's camera, upon which the web page the QR Code is linked to opens in the device's browser window. There are many free barcode scanner apps available for iOS- and Android-based devices and Windows-based tablets. When planning a lesson using websites and/or apps, using a QR Code eliminates student errors in entering URLs or finding specific apps. It makes the search for data quick and easy.

Figure 2.3. Example of a QR Code

Source: www.qr-code-generator.com.

A NOTE ABOUT TIME

One of the first things you might notice when collecting real-time data is that often the events being reported seem to be happening in the future. For example, when looking at USGS real-time data at 6:00 p.m. Eastern Standard Time (EST) on December 29, the data might show a seismic event to have happened after 10:00 p.m. that evening—four hours later than now. Similarly, the National Oceanic and Atmospheric Administration (NOAA) buoy data also might be from nearly 10:00 p.m. that evening. These discrepancies in time do not mean these events are predicted; rather, they are events that have already occurred but are reported in Coordinated Universal Time (UTC).

When working with real-time data, take some time to explain to students that scientists report all data, including planetary data, using UTC to synchronize recorded events. UTC is a 24-hour system of time zones that move outward from the Prime Meridian. UTC is fixed and does not adjust seasonally; for example, for daylight savings time. Having a standard for reporting is important. Scientists are often geographically separated and use data collected from different locations. Recording events using a standard timekeeping system makes data more useful. Table 2.1 shows the time differences between UTC and other U.S. time zones.

Table 2.1. UTC conversion to U.S. time zones

U.S. Time Zone	EST	EDT	CST	CDT	MST	MDT	PST	PDT
Difference from UTC (hour)	–5	–4	–6	–5	–7	–6	–8	–7

CST = Central Standard Time	MST = Mountain Standard Time
CDT = Central Daylight Time	MDT = Mountain Daylight Time
EST = Eastern Standard Time	PST = Pacific Standard Time
EDT = Eastern Daylight Time	PDT = Pacific Daylight Time

Calculating the UTC depends on where you are and what time of the year it is. In the winter, UTC is eight hours later than Pacific Standard Time (PST), while Pacific Daylight time is only seven hours later. As long as students are accessing data and working with real-time data, the time difference is not a problem. Unless they are using their own data with a real-time data set, they will always be comparing data using the same system. It is worth making sure that your students understand that the times in the data are not the same as local time. Should you ever need to convert UTC time to local time, there are many online calculators that can help with the conversion.

MANAGING DEVICES

Although smartphones and tablets are becoming more common in all sections of society, not all students will have access to one. No student should ever feel disadvantaged or left out for not having a device. Even students who have their own devices might have restrictions that prevent them from downloading or accessing data. Teachers generally know their students and can plan accordingly. If approximately half of the students in a class bring a personal smartphone or tablet, that is more than enough to conduct investigations with real-time data using student devices. Although a few will find some reason why they cannot look up the data or download an app, even though they can easily enough send text messages, students can share and conduct their investigations in small groups, rather than individually. Also, in many areas, device availability is not a problem because many school districts now provide tablets for classroom use. If this is not the case for your district, the data we discuss here also can be accessed using laptop or desktop computers. According to the Pew Research Center (Lenhart 2015), more than half of American teenagers currently have access to and use smartphones. That means that most teachers are likely to have enough students in their classes who have devices to allow for easy access to real-time data.

As any teacher of students with smartphones knows, managing those devices in the classroom can be challenging. Students are constantly texting their parents and each other, and seem addicted to social media. If you are using an app, begin the lesson by asking students to start the download and put the phone or tablet face-down in front of them on their desk. You will immediately know how many devices are available for the activity and how to modify your lesson, if necessary. Ask also that all cell phones that do not have the app and are not downloading it be put away.

Donna has found that when students use their devices for interaction with real-time data, they usually stay on task and often report using the app independently on their own time. If you need app settings to be changed, incorporate that into your lesson. If you are providing instructions via a whiteboard presentation, be sure to include some screenshots of the app or website—for iOS devices and many Android devices, this is done by simultaneously holding down the home and power buttons—and email them yourself so you can embed them in your lesson instructions. And of course, remember to use a QR Code to help students find the right app or web page easily.

GRAPHING DATA

After students collect the real-time data for their investigations, they usually are expected to do something evaluative with it; for example, produce a map, chart, or graph. Chapter 4 discusses processing and graphing data in great detail, so we will not go into it here; however, we will cover some technology issues here related to graphing data. Electronic spreadsheets are commonly used for producing graphs. Microsoft Excel is one of the most common spreadsheet programs and is available as an app for iOS and Android platforms. Spreadsheet programs use columns and rows for data entry, and then can create a graph that visually represents those data.

Using spreadsheet programs effectively involves knowing not only what type of graph is best for representing the data, but also how make the program produce that graph. For example, when creating a scatter plot in Excel, it is important to put only numerical data in your two data columns. When creating a bar graph or line graph, though, the data for the *x*-axis must be text; otherwise, the values in both columns will be represented as data bars or points on the graph that is produced (for example, see Figure 2.4). You can display a graph's data table with the graph easily enough by choosing an alternative chart layout. Graphs also can be customized by reversing their axes, inserting data tables and trend lines, and adding axis labels. If you plan to ask students to create a graph using a spreadsheet, be sure to let them know how to set up the data to produce the correct graph.

Figure 2.4. Example of bar graphing done in Microsoft Excel

	A	B	C	D	E	F	G
1	Shirt Size	Number					
2	10	3					
3	12	17					
4	14	22					
5	16	15					
6	18	8					
7	20	4					
8							
9							
10							
11							
12							
13							
14	Shirt Size	Number					
15	ten	3					
16	twelve	17					
17	fourteen	22					
18	sixteen	15					
19	eighteen	8					
20	twenty	4					
21							
22							
23							
24							
25							

Shirts Ordered by Size

	1	2	3	4	5	6
Shirt Size	10	12	14	16	18	20
Number	3	17	22	15	8	4

Shirts Ordered by Size

	ten	twelve	fourteen	sixteen	eighteen	twenty
Number	3	17	22	15	8	4

Another option for producing graphs is to use an app or a website. On websites such as *Datacopia* (*www.datacopia.com*) and *Raw* (*http://app.raw.densitydesign.org*), you can insert raw data into a text box and it will create several graph options for those data. Some of these sites use responsive design, meaning they will reformat their interface to work easily on devices with different screen sizes. This option is great for simple data sets, but is not appropriate if you want to produce more-complex data visualizations. For example, such sites do not allow the axes to be reversed. Also, to select the correct visualization from those the site generates, students must understand which of the graphs produced is the most appropriate. Some free apps are available as well, such as *Graph* for iOS and *Free Graph* for Android. *Google Sheets* is also available as a free app and can be used on both platforms.

If you are working with younger students, there are learning benefits from having the students manually enter the data into tables (as discussed in Chapter 4) and graph it. In these cases, teachers can use a scaffolding approach (providing them partially to fully designed table and graph templates) before having them drawing the tables and graphs by hand on blank paper. In addition, the website *Create-a-Graph* (*https://nces.ed.gov/nceskids/createeagraph*) is designed for younger students and can help them produce graphs (although we would still encourage them to learn the fundamentals first through graphing by hand).

SUMMARY

In this chapter, we have discussed many of the technological aspects of retrieving and processing real-time data. Not all classrooms will look the same; many teachers have labs that use desktops, laptops, and even portable tablets. Many teachers will take advantage of the BYOT devices students bring with them to class and transform those smartphones and tablets into authentic learning tools by using them to access real-time data. Whatever tools you need to use in your classroom, we hope you found information here that will help you identify and manage the technology issues that might arise as your students engage in investigations using real-time data.

REFERENCES

Bosco, J. 2013. Rethinking acceptable use policies to enable digital learning: A guide for school districts. Washington, DC: Consortium for School Networking. *www.cosn.org/sites/default/files/pdf/Revised%20AUP%20March%202013_final.pdf*.

Lenhart, A. 2015. Teens, Social media and technology overview 2015. Washington, DC: Pew Research Center. *www.pewinternet.org/2015/04/09/teens-social-media-technology-2015*.

Savchenko, V. 2014. *Weather History Explorer* app. Sofia, Bulgaria.

U.S. Geological Survey (USGS). *Earthquake hazards program. http://earthquake.usgs.gov/earthquakes/map*.

3

CONDUCTING INVESTIGATIONS
WITH REAL-TIME DATA

Before the internet brought us into the Information Age, teachers often depended on current events to bring their students valuable teachable moments. News stories about an earthquake half a world away or a local weather event would have provided an authentic learning opportunity that actively engaged students. But access to real-world investigations was limited geographically and temporally—unless an event was "newsworthy" and received media coverage, it was not easily available for investigation. Access to real-time data has opened up a world of authentic learning experiences that require analysis skills and critical thinking. Using real-time data sets in student investigations is more challenging than using data sets from textbooks; however, the experience is more motivating to students and allows them to experience higher achievement (McKay and McGrath 2006).

Classroom investigations that use real-time data have characteristics that can make them more challenging for both the student and the teacher. They often involve problems and problem solving that are ill-structured, complex, dynamic, and collaborative (McKay and McGrath 2006). Complex problems such as investigations using real-time data contain large and diverse number elements that are interconnected (Funke 2010). Because data are continuously collected and reported, each data set is dynamic, and the investigation one day might be different from the investigation the day before or after it. The questions could change, and the answers would shift with each new exploration.

Working with real-time data develops deeper understanding of concepts because the data are not always neat and clean, and sometimes are incomplete. For instance, when students gather streamflow data to investigate relationships between precipitation and stream discharge, they might find that some information is missing and other information is irrelevant to their investigation. Students will need to apply their understanding of potential variables to conduct their investigation, and then justify their results to others in a collaborative environment.

LEVELS OF INQUIRY

It is important that students be scaffolded into these real-time data activities in a way that increases the likelihood of their success in their investigation. All too often, we have seen teachers engage their students through opposite extremes—either giving them far too many instructions, such that all students are doing the same investigation with the same data set, or giving them no instructions, so that they flounder and have difficulty deciding what to do with what data. Teachers should use their knowledge of their students to decide how best to engage them.

Traditional science investigations can be broken down into different components, and often are taught as step-by-step activities that give students effectively no leeway in the investigation; however, that is not the type of investigation we are promoting in this book. Tamir (1991) suggested an approach to conducting laboratory investigations that moves students toward working more independently and thus helps them develop better critical-thinking and problem-solving skills. His approach comprises four levels of inquiry in the science laboratory (Table 3.1), which we believe is a good starting point for thinking about this issue.

Table 3.1. Tamir's (1991) levels of inquiry in the science laboratory

Level of Inquiry	Problems	Procedures	Conclusions
0	Given	Given	Given
1	Given	Given	Open
2	Given	Open	Open
3	Open	Open	Open

Teachers tend to interpret information such as that in Table 3.1 as meaning that students can do anything they want; however, that is not how we propose you use it. Rather, it is a structure by which an investigation might be varied to add interest and/or complexity. As an example, say you have a topic you want them to investigate (for example, what is it like for a marine bird to live in the ocean ecosystem) and resources you want them to use (for example, buoys on the Atlantic coast of the United States). In a traditional investigation activity (that is, Level 0) students all address the same question (for example, What is the wave action like at Buoy x at date/time y?) and are expected to get the same answer. A Level 1 activity might have all students use the same sampling approach and answer the same question but let each group choose what buoy's data they investigate. A Level 2 activity might let each group develop their own sampling approach and defend it to others (but with everyone using data from the same buoy). A Level 3 approach might allow groups to ask their own question, for example, "What is the relationship between wave action and closeness to shore?"

Tamir's method can also be used to differentiate activities to allow students with different academic needs to work on different investigations using the same data set. Some teachers allow students to look at Tamir's table and pick the activity level they are comfortable doing.

An advantage of using this framework for helping the students design their own investigations is that each group will have its own data set and argument to present to others for discussion—which is exactly what scientists do when they present their research at conferences. Figure 3.1 shows wind, wave, temperature, and other ocean-conditions data from a National Data Buoy Center (NDBC) buoy near Breezy Point, New York. Using these data, what type of investigation could your students conduct at each of Tamir's levels of inquiry?

Figure 3.1. Buoy data for ocean conditions on January 20, 2016, near Breezy Point, New York

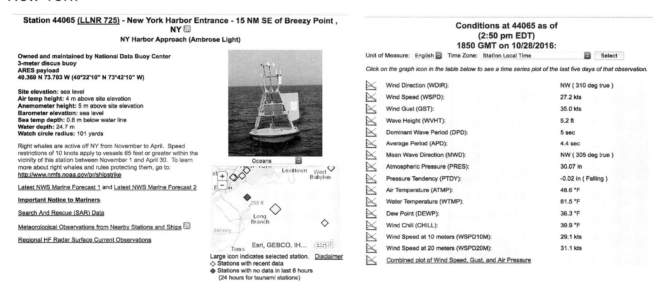

Source: National Data Buoy Center. *www.ndbc.noaa.gov/station_page.php?station=44065.*

DISTINGUISHING BETWEEN INVESTIGATIONS AND EXPERIMENTS

In school labs, students are most accustomed to performing experiments, procedures in which they manipulate one variable (such as temperature) to see what effect it has on another variable (such as solubility). This type of research examines the *causal* relationship between the variables. For example, in an experiment involving temperature and solubility, students would find that temperature affects solubility, and in their conclusion, could claim this relationship. The causal nature of the relationship can be seen directly.

Most of the investigations in this book focus on relationships between the variables being examined. Causality (one variable causing the other to change) is hard to determine and, at best, it can be only inferred if a number of conditions are met (see Bowen and

Bartley 2014 for details). For instance, in an investigation examining wind speed (measured by buoys) and distance from the shore, we divide the buoys' proximity to shore into three ranges: close, medium, and far. These data can help us to determine the relationship between wind speed and distance from shore, but not that one variable caused the other.

Investigations can be categorized as two types—*primary* and *secondary*—by looking at the source of the data. Investigations that are designed to collect and then analyze data are often referred to as primary investigations. Those that use data collected by others are known as secondary investigations. This book's investigations are almost all secondary investigations because students will use data collected by others.

Because this book's investigations use secondary data, students must do their best to understand several things about the data being collected, including

- how the original investigators are using the data,

- how the data are being collected, and

- what the limitations of those data might be.

Understanding these issues, particularly the last two, is important for conclusions that students might draw from the data. For instance, wave action can be collected in a number of different ways, some of which are more sensitive than others. If a large floating buoy is used to record wave action, for example, then small waves might not be accurately or completely recorded. Variations in readings from the large buoy might be small waves, or might just be noise. Understanding how data are collected helps to identify limitations of those data and what types of conclusions can be drawn from them.

SCIENCE AND ENGINEERING PRACTICES

When planning investigations using real-time data, you should provide opportunities for students to engage in the science and engineering practices defined in the *Next Generation Science Standards* (*NGSS;* NGSS Lead States 2013) and *A Framework for K–12 Science Education: Practices, Crosscutting Concepts, and Core Ideas* (NRC 2012). These practices actively engage students in the process of science in a way that requires critical-thinking and problem-solving skills. Activities often involve multiple practices that are *not* carried out in isolation from each other and that can be implemented in a range of activities and on any of Tamir's (1991) levels of inquiry. There are multiple ways to use each data set, as well as different levels of support that can be integrated into each investigation. The science and engineering practices identified in the framework are

- Asking questions (for science) and defining problems (for engineering);

- Developing and using models;

- Planning and carrying out investigations;

- Analyzing and interpreting data;

- Using mathematics and computational thinking;

- Constructing explanations (for science) and designing solutions (for engineering);

- Engaging in argument from evidence; and

- Obtaining, evaluating, and communicating information.

ASKING QUESTIONS AND DEFINING PROBLEMS

A somewhat oversimplified way of stating the difference between science and engineering is to say they have a difference in purpose—the process of science addresses "how" and "why" questions to explain the natural world, whereas the process of engineering seeks to solve problems. Real-time data can be used in both disciplines. For example, in a guided exploration of seasonal patterns, students can use real-time data to explore how the length of the solar day changes through the year (Figure 3.2). Because questions often arise from observation, you could ask students to research seasonal changes in the length of the day at different latitudes. In addition, you might ask them to determine whether there is a relationship between climate and the length of the solar day, as well as research what other variables might account for this observed phenomenon.

Figure 3.2. Length of a solar day at different latitudes

	Jan	Feb	Mar	Apr	May	June	July	Aug	Sept	Oct	Nov	Dec
Nairobi 1°S	12:12	12:10	12:08	12:06	12:04	12:03	12:03	12:04	12:05	12:07	12:09	12:11
Pensacola 30°N	10:13	10:45	11:32	12:29	13:21	13:59	14:05	13:35	12:46	11:52	10:58	10:20
Oslo 60°N	6:03	7:59	10:27	13:16	15:57	18:16	18:42	16:51	14:11	11:29	8:44	6:30

Y-axis: **Hours: Minutes** (21:36, 19:12, 16:48, 14:24, 12:00, 9:36, 7:12, 4:48, 2:24, 0:00)

Latitude, Month, and Solar Day Length

Source: U.S. Naval Observatory. *www.usno.navy.mil.*

Because of the ill-structured nature of real-time data, students will discover that there is a correlation between climate and latitude, but will also find that other variables are involved, which will spur other questions. For example, Paris, France, and St. John's, Newfoundland, are at equivalent latitudes, 48°N and 47°N. It seldom snows in Paris, yet St. John's is much colder and gets more than 10 feet of snow per year. So, although the photoperiod of these two locations is the same on any given day, their climates are very different. Just presenting students with differences such as these will generate questions that are perfect for guiding student investigations. Students could also use the data in this example for engineering applications, for example, to identify energy demands and resources needed to solve regional energy supply problems.

DEVELOPING AND USING MODELS

A model, in this context, refers to a conceptual or mental representation of a phenomenon or phenomena. It can include drawings, simulations, and diagrams, but also can include (and usually does, in science) mathematical and graphical representations. Real-time data can be used to construct multiple types of models to help students better visualize and demonstrate scientific phenomena. Creating a graph with real-time data is just one example. Another would be mapping plate movement using real-time data for plate motion.

For example, using the plate-motion calculator on the UNAVCO website (*www.unavco.org/software/geodetic-utilities/plate-motion-calculator/plate-motion-calculator.html*), students can find how fast tectonic plates under various world cities are moving, and construct a map using vectors showing the speed and direction of plate movement. The map produced is a model that can help us to visualize how Earth's crust changes over time. Such a model could be useful as part of an engineering task to determine what geologic stresses should be addressed through building codes for a given location. Real-time data can be used to create a model or to provide a model for analysis and interpretation.

> ## MODELS
>
> In science, models can be terribly complex or very simple. Believe it or not, you already know about the simple type of science model—drawing a scatter plot, fitting the line of best fit, and determining the equation of that line (in the old $y = mx + b$ format) gives you a simple scientific model. But models are really useful when they allow you to *predict* what will happen in a future scenario.

PLANNING AND CARRYING OUT INVESTIGATIONS

The practice of planning and carrying out investigations is the one most easily enacted with real-time data. Planning and carrying out investigations involves describing the world around us and testing explanations about how it works. Exploring an Earth science or environmental science concept involves testing variables and exploring relationships. Sometimes investigations begin with the data. For example, air-quality data for the six pollutants monitored by the Environmental Protection Agency (EPA) can be downloaded from their website into a spreadsheet and graphed (Figure 3.3). Such data can engender research questions for students to investigate. For example:

- What inferences can be made from the data?

- What variables affect the observed variations in the data?

- What additional data need to be collected to determine relationships among variables?

- How can the data be used to support student hypotheses?

- What is the relationship among the levels of the different pollutants (that is, does one go up when another goes down)?

Other times, investigations begin with observations, and real-time data then can provide evidence to test explanations or develop new theories. In engineering, real-time data can help provide important information for design criteria.

Figure 3.3. Air-quality data for Birmingham, Alabama, for 2015

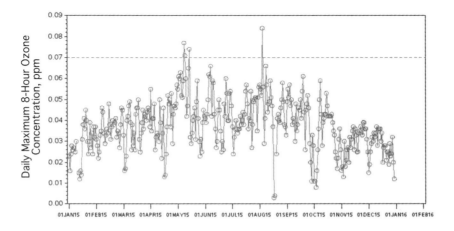

Source: U.S. Environmental Protection Agency. *www.epa.gov/air-data.*

ANALYZING AND INTERPRETING DATA

All real-time data investigations involve analyzing and interpreting data. The instructional challenge is in helping students make sense of those data. Finding the right data, narrowing down very large data sets, and presenting the data in a useful way for analysis are among the many challenges of working with real-time data. So much information is available that it can be overwhelming; however, keep in mind that today's students are part of the digital generation, and can be resourceful in filtering through an abundance of links and resources to find just the right data they need. Sometimes they need to be directed to targeted data resources within a specific website or app.

Table 3.2 shows an example of the how complex data sets can be simplified for students. These data were extracted from a complex set of radiosonde data for Little Rock, Arkansas, for December 22, 2015 (University of Wyoming). A radiosonde is an atmospheric data-collection instrument that often is carried aloft by a weather balloon. The original data set contained 11 columns and more than 300 rows of data and included not just what is in this table, but also air pressure, relative humidity, wind speed, and other information for hundreds of altitudes as the radiosonde ascended. Not all of those data are necessary for students to explore the relationship between altitude and atmospheric temperature. Determining which data are needed is the first factor to consider in an investigation. The second consideration is how to trim the available data set to a manageable size. For example, using every tenth data point is likely sufficient for student investigations. Too much data can overwhelm students (depending on their age and previous knowledge of the subject, of course), and they need to know what to focus on; however, abundant data resources should not necessarily be disregarded, either. By discussing the types of data provided, students might generate new questions for further investigation or discover possible relationships to explore.

Once the data have been found, the most common challenge is what to do with them. Models are one way of visualizing data, and include graphs and charts. Graphing data is one of the most difficult concepts for students to grasp, and is challenging for even the most advanced students. Although rules such as "use line graphs for data over time" and "use bar graphs for comparisons" are generally sound advice, special types of graphs exist that do not fit those rules. Also, these exceptions to the rules can vary greatly by science discipline or subdiscipline. However, that there are general rules (see Chapter 4) as well as discipline-based exceptions does not mean that anything goes. For example, the Stüve profile chart in Figure 3.4 (p. 36) shows a vertical temperature profile of the atmosphere over Little Rock, Arkansas. Knowing what to do to visualize data is not easy, and students will need help with analyzing and interpreting real-time data. Chapter 4 will go into detail on how to help students visualize, analyze, and interpret real-time data. It is important to provide instruction that guides students through the process of analysis and interpretation using discussion, questions, and even direct instruction, whether the purpose of the investigation is to understand a scientific principle or to design an engineering task.

Table 3.2. Radiosonde data from December 22, 2015, for a vertical temperature profile of the atmosphere over Little Rock, Arkansas

Elevation (m)	Temperature (°C)	Dew Point (°C)
173	7.8	5.8
2,288	9.2	−38.8
4,267	−3.1	−41.0
6,134	−18.5	−27.5
8,156	−34.1	−45.1
10,550	−53.1	−69.1
12,364	−64.7	−76.7
14,215	−65.7	−81.7
16,200	−62.7	−87.7
18,215	−62.5	−89.5
20,422	−62.2	−91.3
22,131	−61.1	−92.1
24,265	−59.5	−90.5
26,213	−61.4	−92.3
29,190	−60.5	−91.5
3 1,271	−50.3	−84.3
33,239	−4 7.7	−82.7

Data source: University of Wyoming. *http://weather.uwyo.edu/upperair/sounding.html.*

Using Mathematics and Computational Thinking

From understanding the units used in reporting various data to describing relationships and predicting outcomes, the use of mathematics is the foundation on which real-time data analysis rests. Whether a student is interpreting earthquake magnitude using the logarithmic Richter scale or calculating the rate at which a glacier is retreating, working with real-time data requires mathematical reasoning and computational skills, and the importance of these cannot be overstated. *A Framework for K–12 Science Education: Practices, Crosscutting Concepts, and Core Ideas* (NRC 2012) stresses the role of mathematics in working with data:

Figure 3.4. Stüve diagram of the vertical temperature profile for the atmosphere over Little Rock, Arkansas, plotted with data from Table 3.2

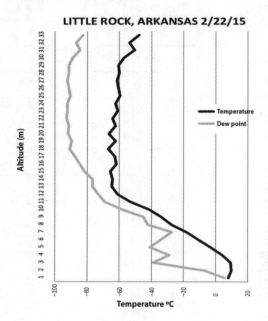

Mathematics (including statistics) and computational tools are essential for data analysis, especially for large data sets. The abilities to view data from different perspectives and with different graphical representations, to test relationships between variables, and to explore the interplay of diverse external conditions all require mathematical skills that are enhanced and extended with computational skills. (NRC 2012, p. 65).

Not all real-time data sets will require advanced calculations. Depending on the activity, students might only need to understand units or orders of magnitude, or be able to calculate slope to understand trends in the data. Seldom will the learning objective be the calculations themselves; rather, it will be to understand how data are used to understand and interpret the world. So when planning an investigation, it is often best to try to simplify the computations and focus instead on the big ideas—using real-time data to investigate Earth's systems and our environment.

CONSTRUCTING EXPLANATIONS (FOR SCIENCE) AND DESIGNING SOLUTIONS (FOR ENGINEERING)

In science, explanations tie together observations, and explanations and data are brought together to develop theories. Data provide evidence that supports scientific understandings. Explanations incorporate data in making inferences, predicting events, and providing evidence for causal relationships. For applications using real-time data, this means letting the data support and reinforce the concepts presented. Whatever those concepts are—a connection between sea-level rise and mean global temperatures, for example, or between land use and population trends—real-time data help students construct explanations.

In investigating the relationship between carbon dioxide (CO_2) and ocean acidification, for example, data from the National Oceanic and Atmospheric Administration (NOAA) (Figure 3.5, p. 38), can provide a model to help students make connections. The graphs in the figure plot the daily data collected by a buoy off the coast of southern California. Since 2012, this buoy has collected data on the pH level of the ocean water and the CO_2 level of the seawater and the atmosphere. There are expected gaps in the data, but trends are clear

> ### THEORY
>
> In science, a theory is a big idea that pulls together broad patterns. Sometimes people talk about *theory* in science as though it means that we do not have enough information. That is, they will say, "Oh, it's just a theory." But that is an incorrect understanding of theory in science. To a scientist, calling something a theory usually means that there is a lot of evidence (that is, data) and that the data are pretty consistent, without any meaningful contradictions.

none the less. The graphs show that as the seawater's CO_2 level increased, its pH level decreased. A decrease in pH means the water has become more acidic.

Such a relationship could be predicted by understanding that when CO_2 mixes with seawater, it forms carbonic acid. This affects sea life in multiple ways, including reducing the availability of carbonate ions, which are used by marine organisms that produce shells. The reduction in pH alone can create problems for sensitive organisms. This investigation is just one example of how real-time data can be used by students to construct explanations in science. Those explanations then become the basis for developing criteria and constraints in engineering design.

ENGAGING IN ARGUMENT FROM EVIDENCE

Engaging in argument from evidence is probably the most useful scientific process for developing conceptual understanding. When students can build a case to support their explanations, they are engaged with content at a deep and meaningful level. Building their case requires supporting evidence, and real-time data can be useful in supporting their claims.

Figure 3.5. Ocean-acidification data for 2016 collected off the coast of California

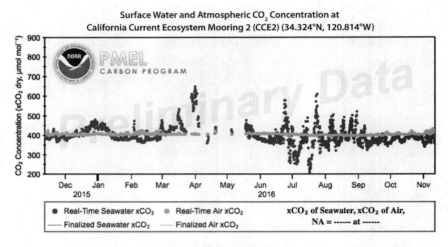

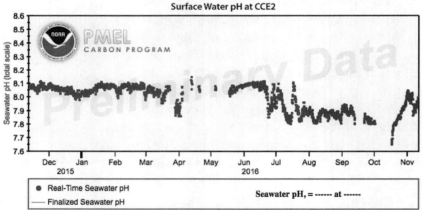

Source: National Oceanic and Atmospheric Administration. *www.pmel.noaa.gov/co2/story/OA+Observations+and+Data.*

Teachers who have implemented argumentation strategies have found that when students are asked to use evidence to support their claims, they are engaged at a deeper level, their thinking processes are evident, and their misconceptions are revealed. Use of real-time data possibly is one of the best resources for students who are asked to develop an argument.

For example, students might be asked to use real-time earthquake data as evidence to support the claim that the Australian Plate is subducting under the Pacific Plate. Using 30-day earthquake data downloaded from the U.S. Geological Survey (USGS), students can locate seismic events along a specific plate boundary (Table 3.3). These data can be narrowed to certain geographic regions at the plate boundaries and then graphed (Figures 3.6 and 3.7, p. 40). Best-fit lines can help students visualize the plate boundary, and show where the deepest events occur along the leading edge of the subducting plate. These data can be used with other evidence, such as plate-motion calculations discussed earlier (Developing and Using Models, p. 32) to provide evidence for the claim that the Australian Plate is subducting under the Pacific Plate.

Table 3.3. USGS 30-day earthquake data for May 19, 2017, through June 10, 2017 (lat = latitude; long = longitude)

Date	Lat S	Long W	Depth (km)	Magnitude
5/19	–19.8	–174.0	14.4	4.5
5/20	–23.9	–179.7	492.1	4.5
5/22	–18.7	–172.7	10.0	5.1
5/22	–24.0	–179.8	530.3	4.6
5/25	–22.4	–176.3	110.2	5.3
5/26	–21.0	–178.7	561.8	5.0
5/29	–21.4	–178.5	554.6	4.6
5/30	–21.4	–176.6	182.1	4.6
6/1	–19.7	–173.4	10.0	4.8
6/5	–21.3	–178.2	448.8	4.5
6/9	–23.1	–176.8	176.8	4.7
6/10	–18.6	–173.1	64.3	4.6

Data source: U.S. Geological Survey. *http://earthquake.usgs.gov.*

This is just one example of using real-time data in constructing arguments. Once students engage in activities involving argumentation, they begin to see that the scientific

Figure 3.6. Earthquake depth versus longitude (Table 3.3 data) at the Pacific–Australian tectonic-plate boundary

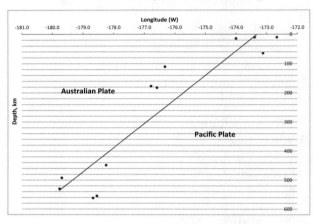

Figure 3.7. Tectonic boundaries

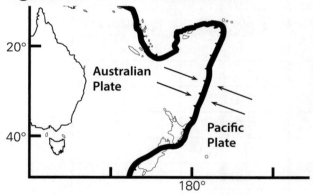

Source: Modified from U.S. Geological Survey map. *https://volcanoes.usgs.gov/about/edu/dynamicplanet/ballglobe/simplifiedmap.pdf.*

world is built on sound, data-supported evidence and start to build their own skills in scientific reasoning. Engineering practices also rely on data to help make choose the best solutions in design decisions.

OBTAINING, EVALUATING, AND COMMUNICATING INFORMATION

Science is a collaborative process and cannot be conducted in isolation. It is a social process; the work done by one scientist is built on by others. For science to progress, one scientist's findings must be communicated and evaluated by other scientists. Whether those findings are supported or rejected by the scientific community, through this process science moves forward. To understand the social nature of science, students must have opportunities to investigate phenomena, communicate their results, and evaluate the findings of others. Using real-time data in student explorations engages students in an authentic learning experience. Conclusions they make in investigations are based on actual data, not simulations from a fictitious scenario. Events represented by the data can be experienced as they happen in the real world. Obtaining real-time data to support investigations is easier than ever with tablet and smartphone technologies; however, evaluating those data still requires critical-thinking skills and interpretation built on conceptual understandings. The more students engage in these practices, the better grasp they will have of the content and the deeper understanding they will have of how science works.

SUMMARY

In this chapter, we have shown how real-time data can be used to engage students in scientific and engineering practices, as suggested by *A Framework for K–12 Science Education: Practices, Crosscutting Concepts, and Core Ideas* (NRC 2012). Although it is not realistic to incorporate every practice into every investigation, most lessons integrate multiple

NATIONAL SCIENCE TEACHERS ASSOCIATION

practices. At the very least, every investigation with real-time data will include the practices of obtaining, evaluating, and communicating information; analyzing and interpreting data; and constructing explanations. Visual or graphical models also may be included in most activities. Mathematical thinking, argumentation, planning investigations, and asking questions are also common components of investigations using real-time data. What your students get out of the experience will depend on what criteria you set, what questions you ask, and what problems students are expected to solve. To help your students understand the data they are using, it would be helpful to explore types of data and ways to process them, and how to graph real-time data (see Chapter 4).

REFERENCES

Bowen, G. M., and A. Bartley. 2014. *The basics of data literacy: Helping your students (and you!) make sense of data.* Arlington, VA: NSTA Press.

Funke, J. 2010. Complex problem solving: a case for complex cognition? *Cognitive Processing* 11 (2): 133–142.

McKay, M., and B. McGrath. 2006. Real world problem-solving using real time data. *International Journal of Engineering Education* 23 (1): 36–41.

National Oceanic and Atmospheric Administration (NOAA). National Data Buoy Center. *www.ndbc.noaa.gov/station_page.php?station=44065.*

National Oceanic and Atmospheric Administration (NOAA). PMEL Carbon Program. *www.pmel.noaa.gov/co2/story/OA+Observations+and+Data.*

National Research Council (NRC). 2012. *A framework for K–12 science education: Practices, crosscutting concepts, and core ideas.* Washington, DC: National Academies Press.

NGSS Lead States. 2013. *Next Generation Science Standards: For states, by states.* Washington, DC: National Academies Press. *www.nextgenscience.org/next-generation-science-standards.*

Tamir, P. 1991. Practical work in school science: An analysis of current practice. In *Practical science*, ed. B. E. Woolnough, 13–20. Milton Keynes, England: Open University Press.

UNAVCO Corporation. 2016. Plate motion calculator widget. *www.unavco.org/software/geodetic-utilities/plate-motion-calculator/plate-motion-calculator.html.*

University of Wyoming, Department of Atmospheric Science. Upperair air data: Soundings. *http://weather.uwyo.edu/upperair/sounding.html.*

U.S. Environmental Protection Agency. AirData. *www.epa.gov/air-data.*

U.S. Geological Survey. Dynamic Planet. *https://volcanoes.usgs.gov/about/edu/dynamicplanet/ballglobe/simplifiedmap.pdf.*

U.S. Geological Survey. *Earthquake Hazards Program. http://earthquake.usgs.gov.*

U.S. Naval Observatory. *www.usno.navy.mil.*

4

DATA TYPES, REPRESENTATION, AND ANALYSIS

The data sets discussed in this book are very different in many ways from the types of data that are normally used in schools. The biggest difference is that these data sets can be huge—thousands and thousands of numbers—almost too big to deal with, and so require different handling than the data students more typically use in school. Their size and complexity necessitate that students make different kinds of decisions in using them, decisions that students are more than capable of making.

As an example, imagine students asking the question "What is the wind speed along an ocean coast?" Researching this question would involve a large data set, and so students also would need to ask "When?" because the data could contain tens of thousands of measurements over many years. They also would need to ask "Where?" because those tens of thousands of measurements could include hundreds of places that wind speed is measured on ocean coasts. Helping

HOW MANY SAMPLES OR REPLICATES?

A question to be considered in every study is how many samples or replicates are needed. Whether you use samples or replicates will depend on your study. For example, for the wind-speed question in the discussion, the sample is the number of sites you choose along the coast (for example, 10 locations), and the replicate is the number of data points, the number of times you collect data from each of those sites (for example, every data point in one week, once a week for 52 weeks). On the other hand, you could also sample 1,000 spots along the coast just once. Students often collect the number as instructed by a teacher; however, this does not really represent what happens in real-world science. The number of samples or replicates in real-world science is often based on (a) what is possible time- and money-wise, (b) the researchers' judgement of whether the (suspected) range of possible data has been adequately represented, and/or (c) whether the number of samples/replicates will be convincing to other researchers.

students learn to narrow their question to a manageable scope is important for their success in working with real-time data.

There are many solutions that help students refocus their questions; these usually help the students reframe their research question into a more specific focus, e.g, narrowing the wind-speed question above to evaluate a few specific coastal locations and/or a specific time of day rather than the 24-hour period. With the research question framed this way, students might then collect data for wind speed measured at noon on one day at 10 random sites along a coast. Or, they might pick 10 specific places (known as a *purposive sample*) and collect the data for a given time every day for a seven-day period. Or, they might use wind-speed data obtained every hour for one week in February and one week in August to compare the mean (arithmetically averaged) wind speed in different seasons. The answers that the students get to their questions depend on such decisions about the specificity of their approach. There really is no right or wrong to those decisions (unless the teacher has made specific requests).

A multitude of questions could be asked, and you can help each student group set an analytic task that is based on data samples with which they can be successful. A group of on-target students could do more data points in all four seasons; another group could do wind speed at noon daily at one location over a month. Your highest-achieving students could compare wind speeds and temperatures over a year (that is, look at whether wind speed and temperature correlate). Helping students develop a focused research question that they can deal with successfully takes a bit of time, but it reduces problems in the analysis and conclusion-drawing stages of their investigations. Once students have collected their data subset, they must decide what they need to do with it to analyze it so that they will be able to show others what they found (that is, to describe their findings and make sense of them). Scientists use tables and graphs to help accomplish all of these tasks, and the following part of this chapter is about helping students learn to do that, as well.

This chapter outlines some of the basic data types that are used in investigations and discusses how to represent and then analyze those data variables in tables and graphs. It provides a general background in data analysis that can improve the effectiveness of the student investigations and the conclusions students draw from them using the activities in this book. It also discusses a specific approach that scientists use in describing their findings, that is, their use of hedging language in talking about the patterns in a data set and the conclusions that can be drawn from the research. Finally, it discusses some types of data that are exceptions to the rule when calculating arithmetic means.

This focus on constructing appropriate data tables and graphs might seem "old school," but time and again we have seen students jotting data down randomly on a page or writing narrative observations while they are collecting them, rather than placing them in an appropriately designed table. In real-world science, data tables are used by researchers to allow them to visually inspect the data for patterns and trends *as they are collecting the data*. This visual inspection partly allows a judgment to be made about whether a particular value is an outlier (one that deviates notably from the overall pattern) that might need to be re-collected or ignored (both of which are common practice in science for outlier data points), or whether there are other implications that should be noted. Some scientists say they look for patterns by mentally drawing a graph of the data as they collect them in data tables.

In this chapter, we describe table structures used with different types of data variables and describe how these facilitate data analysis and the emerging understanding of the phenomena being studied in the research project. Helping students structure effective data tables (for example, by the teacher checking the tables in advance and providing advice on their structure) at the data collection/sampling stage is useful, because having the data organized properly early on helps students with their overall research analysis. Students will have fewer problems with data analysis if they have structured their data tables well.

Graphing software programs make it seem that there are dozens, if not hundreds, of different graph types; however, in science, most disciplines tend to use three main types: bar graphs, line graphs, and scatter plots. Other types also are used sometimes, but we will start with those three. Graphs are used in most science reports that involve quantitative data and are important in science because they summarize large data sets and show data trends very efficiently—which allows patterns to be better understood. As judges of science fair projects, we have noted that students frequently use the wrong type of graph to represent their data, which often leads to misinterpretation of those data and incorrect conclusions. When the right type of graph is used to present data, it tells the right story, which is important when working with primary or secondary data.

VARIABLES

Variables are human-defined. They are identified and defined as part of the process of investigating an observed phenomenon, as a way of making sense of that observation. Scientists identify and define variables as part of the process of formally investigating an observed phenomenon. For instance, after watching lizards in the wild, a herpetologist might want to figure out whether the size of lizards is related to how far they are from a forest's edge. This would require the scientist to define *forest's edge* so that the measurement could be made from there to where the lizard was caught. But how then to actually define *forest's edge*? Sometimes boundaries between habitats are abrupt, but many times are not. For example, habitat borders can have gaps that contain yet other habitats. Defining variables is essential to conducting scientific investigations, but it is often harder to do than it might at first seem.

UNDERSTANDING THE DIFFERENT TYPES OF DATA

Students and teachers often find data analysis difficult because the different types, or orders, of data variables are rarely taught or explicitly discussed and so are often not well understood. Data types are not usually taught in high school or in university science classes, but understanding them—and there are basically only three—can make data analysis much more straightforward. When Mike has given presentations on this at teacher conferences, he has experienced high school teachers who have been teaching for over 20 years tell him they had never known about these distinctions, and that knowing them now has made data and analysis much clearer to them. Understanding the basic types of independent (that is, *x*-axis or causal) data provides a framework for making decisions about how to visualize and analyze them. There are three basic types of data variables, each with specific characteristics and a type of graph usually used to represent it: *nominal* data (informally called *category* data), *ordinal* data (*ordered category* data), and *interval–ratio*[1] data (*measured* data).

Table 4.1. Temperatures recorded at 10 cities each on the East and West Coasts at noon local time on February 10, 2015 (fictional data)

City	Temperature (°C)	
	East Coast	West Coast
1	6	14
2	9	8
3	8	8
4	7	7
5	10	11
6	9	12
7	7	11
8	9	9
9	6	9
10	10	13
Mean	8.1	10.2

NOMINAL (CATEGORY) VARIABLE

The simplest sort of variable is the nominal variable, also known as a category variable. Nominal variables have no intrinsic order. As an example of this, say you want to answer a question such as "Is wind speed greater in the morning or in the afternoon?" "Is the wind speed greater in the spring or the fall?" or "Is wind speed greater on the Pacific or Atlantic side of the United States?" In each case, the dependent variable is wind speed and the independent variable (which in this case is nominal) is the category being compared (time of day, time of year, or geographic location, respectively). Because nominal variables have no order of importance, in these examples, the variables in each pair—morning and afternoon, spring and fall, western United States and eastern United States—would have the same level of importance. This example uses only two components, but you could have many more. For instance, the question "What is the mean wind speed in the middle of each state?" is nominal-level, even though it involves 50 U.S. states as independent variables.

---

1. The interval–ratio data type combines the interval and ratio data types. For the purposes of our discussion here, the difference between these data types is more or less immaterial. By one definition, interval data have a zero, but it does not necessarily mean anything in the big picture, whereas in "ratio" data the zero has meaning (for example, the distinction between 0°C [the freezing point of water only] and 0 kg of mass [which applies to all matter]. However, 0 Kelvin is a "ratio" variable because it refers to a state of molecular movement in all matter.)

In the following example using nominal data, we address the research question "What is the mean noontime temperature in late winter in cities on the east and west coasts of the United States?" To answer this, we picked a date (February 10, 2015) and 10 cities on each coast. We then obtained the data for each city from the internet and record it in a table (see example in Table 4.1).

The structure of Table 4.1 allows a researcher to scan the numbers to identify data anomalies (either a real difference in the data or a problem stemming from the data entry), and to visually compare the means calculated in the table. Even before graphing the data, a researcher might already be drawing tentative conclusions, for example, "the mean temperature for East Coast cities seems to be slightly lower than for West Coast cities." Students often draw a false conclusion from tables such as this one, because they mistakenly think that the data values in the various columns on a given row are related to each other because they are on the same row. However, the data in this type of table are nominal-level, and so data items on the same row are not related to each other. In Table 4.1, for example, because the data are nominal-level, the recorded temperature for City 1 for the East Coast cities is unrelated to recorded temperature for City 1 for the West Coast cities.

Figure 4.1. Mean temperature for 10 cities each on the East and West Coasts on February 10, 2015 (fictional data)

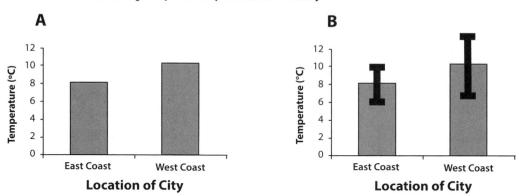

Nominal-level data are often represented in a bar graph or a histogram (which is used for frequencies). Pie charts can be used, but are less common in science publications. When graphing nominal-level data, it is common to use only the mean response, although there are good arguments saying that graphing the raw data as well as the mean allows students to draw conclusions more like those drawn in real-world science (Bowen and Bartley 2014). Note that Figure 4.1 (A) clearly shows a difference between the cities on the two coasts on that day at noon. An acceptable conclusion might be, "On average, temperatures recorded in cities on the West Coast of the United States in mid-February of 2015 were higher than those in cities on the East Coast." It would be even better to conclude, "The arithmetic mean of temperatures recorded in cities on the West Coast of the United States in mid-February of 2015 was higher than that of temperatures recorded in cities on the East Coast."

It is also common in science—and usually expected—to not only compare the mean values, but also comment on how the data scatter around the arithmetic mean (see Bowen and Bartley [2014] for more details on doing this visually and statistically) because this allows researchers to discuss the importance of the amount of the difference. One simple way of doing this that provides additional information is to compare the range of the data (difference between the highest and lowest measurements) to their mean. In the current example (Table 4.1), the East Coast cities have a temperature range of 4°C , and the West Coast cities have a range of 7°C. Figure 4.1 (B) illustrates this comparison of the range of the data in relation to the means by drawing a line representing 4°C and 7°C vertically across the respective means at the top of each bar (that is, 2 degrees above and below the East Coast bar, and 3.5 degrees above and below the West Coast bar). In our example, the difference between the mean temperatures of the West Coast cities and East Coast cities is 2.1°C (that is, 10.2°C minus 8.1°C). The sizes of the ranges in Figure 4.1 (B) suggest that there is considerable data overlap, which means that the temperatures for at least some cities on one coast were similar to temperatures in some cities on the other coast. This, then, might change our conclusion to the following:

> In mid-February of 2015, the mean recorded temperature in cities on the U.S. West Coast was higher than in cities on the U.S. East Coast; however, there was a lot of overlap, which means that several cities on each coast had temperatures that were similar to those of cities on the other coast.

Examining the extent of the overlap of the raw data (for which scientists use the standard deviation and a *t*-test; see Bowen and Bartley 2014) allows you to make stronger statements about differences between means. Also, these nominal-level data allow you to make statements about the data that were measured, but not to make predictions. For instance, the data in Table 4.1 cannot be used to predict the noon temperature in cities on the U.S. Gulf Coast. Remember, nominal-level data do not allow you to make many types of predictions that you could test, other than for the existing categories you looked at.

CATEGORIES OF "DISTANCE FROM SHORE"

Why might a teacher use ordinal categories of distance from shore in a lesson instead of absolute measures of distance? One possible reason is that a teacher is working with younger students. In such a case, one group of students could figure out "nearshore" data, another group "medium distance from shore," and a third group "far from shore." Each group could report its findings to the class, and then the teacher could help the whole class work to understand the "big picture" by combining and evaluating the three groups' findings.

ORDINAL (ORDERED CATEGORY) VARIABLE

The next level of variable is the ordinal variable, also known as an ordered category variable. Ordinal variables can be ordered, for example, small, medium, large, and extra-large coffee cups. However, although they have an intrinsic order, these categories are not consistent multiples of each other, for example, the volume of two small cups of coffee does not necessarily equal the volume of a medium cup. Another way of thinking about the ordinal variable is that it is comparative. "Medium" is variable in meaning. For example, one coffee shop's medium coffee cup might not hold the same volume as another coffee shop's medium cup. Nevertheless, both are "medium" size because each shop also sells smaller and larger cups of coffee.

Figure 4.2. Locations of buoys collecting wave-height data near Seattle, Washington, on February 10, 2015 (fictional data)

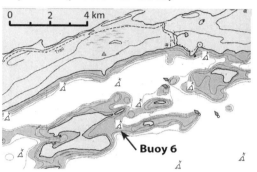

Using the example of wave height, students could examine the difference in mean wave height between locations nearshore, a medium distance from shore, and far from shore. To do this, they would need to define the distance from shore for each of those distance categories. These would have to be distance ranges rather than exact distances because buoys in different locations vary in distance from shore. In this case, students might define "nearshore" as 1 kilometer or less from the mainland shore, "medium distance from the shore" as 1–5 kilometers out, and "far from shore" as 5–10 kilometers out. What is important here is that students must define the categories they want to compare (just like "defining the forest's edge," mentioned earlier). Also, the independent variable "distance from shore" is ordinal-level because it is not a measure, but rather is one of three distance categories ordered from small to large (and note that these are not necessarily *even* distances from shore). Figure 4.2 shows three buoys that are 1 kilometer or less from shore, five that are 1–5 kilometers out, and two that are 5–10 kilometers out. Each buoy would have wind-speed measurements associated with it. The data-table design for ordinal-level data is like that for nominal-level data, except that (a) whereas for a nominal-level study, the data are in different categories (for example, cats and dogs as two categories of animal), for an ordinal-level study, the data are all in the same category (for example, cats of different relative size); and (b) the columns are ordered, usually increasing from left to right.

Using the buoy-distance example and map in Figure 4.2, Table 4.2 (p. 50) can be constructed by measuring the distances using the scale on the map and recording them in the three distance categories. The data in Table 4.2 address the research question, "What is the relationship between distance from shore and height of the waves so we can determine where it is safe to go sailing in a small boat?" To do this, we had to determine where

Table 4.2. Mean wave height at buoys at various distances from the shore on February 10, 2015, near Seattle, Washington (fictional data)

Buoy Sample Number	Mean Wave Height (m)*		
	Nearshore	Medium Distance From Shore	Far From Shore
1	0.5	1.1	4.3
2	0.75	2.3	6.2
3	0.6	0.5	—
4	—	2.9	—
5	—	1.7	—
Mean	0.62	1.7	5.25
*Note how the mean values for individual buoys match the values in the "Mean" row in Table 4.3.			

we wanted to see this relationship (we chose the Seattle area as a hypothetical example), whether we would use ranges of distance (we did use ranges), and whether we would use measures for one specific time or for a mean of the range of wave heights for a time period (we used the mean). We used mean wave heights, so we could demonstrate the use of another table (Table 4.3) to list and calculate the mean of the many samples from a time period to then put into Table 4.2. We chose mean wave height rather than wave height at a specific time because of the research question we were addressing. In this instance, our research question was related to sailing in a small boat, which takes place over a range of time. We calculated the mean for the wave heights over the period from 6:00 a.m. to 6:00 p.m., the dawn-to-dusk time during which someone might go sailing.

When looking at Table 4.2, note these aspects:

- The three distance categories are listed in increasing order from left to right.

- Each distance category has a different number of buoys. This influences how one discusses the conclusions that can be drawn about mean wave height because when there are more sampling locations, you can be more certain about the mean calculated from them. In this case, then, we can be more certain about the mean wave height a medium distance from shore than about the mean wave height far from shore.

The mean values for each buoy sample in Table 4.2 were calculated from the raw data of wave heights recorded at each hour from 6 a.m. to 6 p.m. Table 4.3 lists some of these raw

Table 4.3. Wave height at buoys at different distances from the shore on February 10, 2015, near Seattle, Washington (fictional data)

| Buoy Sample Number | Wave Height (m) and Distance Category | | | | | | | |
| | Nearshore | | | Medium Distance from Shore | | | Far from Shore | |
	1	2	3	1	*	5	1	2
Time					*			
6:00 a.m.	0.45	0.4	0.4	1.2	*	2.5	4.3	5.1
7:00 a.m.	0.3	0.3	0.8	0.8	*	2.1	4.2	5.6
8:00 a.m.	0.6	0.6	0.9	0.9	*	1.7	4.1	5.7
*	*	*	*	*	*	*	*	*
6:00 p.m.	0.6	0.9	0.8	1.0	*	2.1	5.5	8.7
Mean†	0.5	0.75	0.6	1.1	*	1.7	4.3	6.2

*Time rows and buoy sample columns omitted for display purposes.

†Note how these mean wave height values correspond to the mean values for individual buoys in Table 4.2.

data, and then presents the mean of the raw data for each buoy sample at each location. Table 4.2 lists these mean values again, and then their mean, for each location, which allows the research question to be addressed.

In science, ordinal-level data are often represented using a line graph in which a line joins the mean values of each category. In analyses, users usually can obtain more information from a line graph than from a bar graph. In some cases, however, this type of data is depicted in a bar graph (we will discuss this exception below). The common way to graph ordinal-level data is shown in Figure 4.3, which was generated using the data from Table 4.2. Note that in the line graph, the mean wave heights were plotted and joined by a line.

Figure 4.3. Mean wave height recorded by buoys on February 10, 2015, near Seattle, Washington (fictional data)

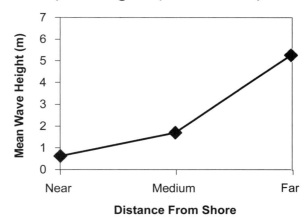

From the graph type in Figure 4.3, a student typically might conclude that mean wave height nearshore is less than that at buoys farther offshore; however, as with the earlier bar graph for nominal-level data, having some idea of the data scatter around each of the means helps in drawing a stronger conclusion. Again, in real-world science, graphs often show measures of data scatter (for example, error bars that represent standard deviation). If, for instance, the data scatter around the means was large for both the nearshore and the medium-distance buoys, then we might be able to conclude that mean wave height was greater far from shore than it was a medium distance from shore and nearshore, but we could not conclude that the medium-distance and nearshore buoys were different.

The graph in Figure 4.4 illustrates scattering, or variation, of data and how it affects interpretation of data in bar graphs and line graphs. The graph shows data for six buoys at which wave heights were determined at one point in the morning and at one point in the afternoon. Mean wave height is shown by the bars; the points represent individual recordings.

Figure 4.4. Bar graph showing scattering of data for wave height measured in the morning and afternoon for Buoy A and Buoy B

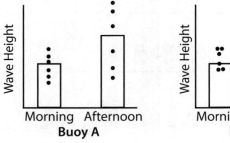
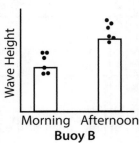

Each point on the graphs represent a single wave-height measurement; i.e. the raw data. In *A*, the data points from the morning are spread out evenly and reasonably tightly around the mean (the bar) in the morning, but the data points from the afternoon are very spread out. We could interpret this as showing that, although the mean of wave heights recorded in the morning was less than that of wave heights recorded in the afternoon, this difference was not true of some individual waves. In contrast, in *B*, the data points show that the heights of all the individual waves were consistently higher in the afternoon than in the morning, such that none of the data points in the two bars overlapped in their range. From this, we could conclude from *B* that the mean wave height recorded by buoys in the afternoon was greater than the mean height of waves recorded in the morning, and that this trend was consistent among all the individual waves measured. Therefore, *B* provides stronger evidence to claim a relationship between wave height and the time of day than *A* does, because the data in *A* show exceptions to the claim, as seen by the overlap of the data ranges. (As noted above, this interpretation of the scatter also can be applied to line graphs.)

However, as mentioned earlier, there are exceptions to the use of the line graph for ordinal data. In some science disciplines, a bar graph is used to depict the relationship between the ordered categories. We encourage you to have your students use the standard practices of whatever science discipline they are working in, although we think that for depicting ordinal-level data, the line-graph approach provides more information in how it shows the differences between the means; with a sloping line between the data points.

INTERVAL–RATIO (MEASURED) VARIABLE

The final type of variable is the interval–ratio variable, also known as a measured variable. This is the highest-order variable type, because complex interpretations can be done from measured variables (we will give an example later in this section. Data of this type must be proportional. For example, two times a 10 km/h wind speed is 20 km/h, and three times a 20 km/h wind speed is 60 km/h, which is six times the 10 km/h (two times multiplied by three times equals six times). Another way of thinking about it is that the differences are identical, for example, wind speed going from 10 km/h to 20 km/h is the same amount of change as going from 100 km/h to 110 km/h. Notice how this is different from the coffee cup example, where the difference in volume between a small and medium cup is not necessarily the same as between a large and an extra-large. Interval–ratio variables are consistently proportional; they also are the most frequent form of variable used in science because they provide the most information for making predictions that can be further tested. We are also quite used to this type of data. The everyday measures we use—volume, mass, speed, temperature—are all interval–ratio variables, whether they are given in metric or U.S. customary units of measurement.

Interval–ratio data require a slightly different table design. This type of data variable compares a measured value (the independent variable) to a measured value (the dependent variable), so it is composed of pairs of numbers. For instance, comparing the mean arm length to the mean leg length of students in a seventh-grade class would be an interval–ratio study. We also can use interval–ratio data with our study of wave height versus distance from shore to understand that relationship differently, by using the measured distances at

OUTLIERS

Earlier, we discussed how scientists often try to identify outliers at the data-entry stage by looking for data-entry and data-collection errors, but they also look for outliers when analyzing graphical representations of the data because sometimes circumstances can cause a valid but aberrant data point. In this case, we recognized the data pair for Buoy 6 (see Table 4.4, p. 54) as an outlier because of the buoy's location, which situated it in a different wind environment from the other buoys. The data pair was excluded from the calculation because such outliers would skew the results from analysis of the research question "What is the relationship between distance from shore and the mean wave height?"

each buoy rather than categories of distance (ordinal data), as we did in the ordinal data analysis example.

To do this, we use the mean wave height (for each hour from 6:00 a.m. to 6:00 p.m.) and the measured distance from the shore for each specific buoy on the map (Figure 4.2, p. 49). Note that data such as measured distances will not necessarily be provided directly by a data source, and in this case, the distance of each buoy from shore was determined by using a ruler to measure the distance on the map and converting that measurement to a real distance using the map scale. The determined distance for each buoy then is recorded in an *x-y* table (Table 4.4, column 1). In essence, at times, students might have to create data such as these, using graphical information such as maps provided with the real-time data set downloaded from the source.

Table 4.4. Mean wave height and distance from shore on February 10, 2015, near Seattle, Washington (fictional data)

Buoy Number	Distance From Shore (km)	Mean Wave Height (m)
1	0.45	0.5
2	0.50	0.75
3	0.43	0.6
4	1.1	1.1
5	1.8	2.3
6	3.1	0.5
7	2.8	1.7
8	2.6	2.9
9	6.0	4.3
10	5.5	6.2

Each "Buoy Number" (Table 4.4, column 1) refers to a specific buoy on the map (Figure 4.2), and the table shows the distance from shore for that buoy and the mean wave height. To reiterate, the distances from the shore in this table were measured on the map using a ruler and the *scale provided on the map*; they would not necessarily be provided directly as measurements from a website itself. This is an example of the type of data that a student would have to create from the information provided at the real-time data set website.

When you examine the data set in the table, notice that one pair of numbers (Buoy 6) seems "off," that is, it is a great distance from shore but has a very low mean wave height.

Because of that, this number pair is an outlier; however, in this case, it does not appear to represent a data error, but rather varies greatly from the overall data pattern because of how "distance from the mainland shore" is defined for this study. As shown on the map (Figure 4.2, p. 49), Buoy 6 is in the lee of an island and therefore is protected from wind by the island. As a result, it has a lower mean wave height than other buoys of similar distance. Although the data point for Buoy 6 should remain in the data set and be plotted in relevant graphs, it should be excluded from analysis of the relationship between wave height and buoy distance from shore. Such data patterns are difficult to discern from a data table alone, so in science, we create a graphical representation.

Scatter plots are the type of graph usually used with interval–ratio data in science. In scatter plots, the raw data points are individually graphed and then often followed by some sort of averaging or "summarizing" of the patterns shown. This graph type is quite powerful in science because not only does it show you the data that has been collected, but it also allows you predict what *might* be measured in other circumstances; those predictions can then be tested. Scatter plots allow the strength of the relationship between the variables to be determined easily, which allows one to draw better conclusions from the data and better understand their implications. In many science disciplines, this type of graph is the most commonly used, because of these characteristics.

Figure 4.5. Wave height versus buoy distance from shore on February 10, 2015, near Seattle, Washington (plotted using Table 4.4 data)

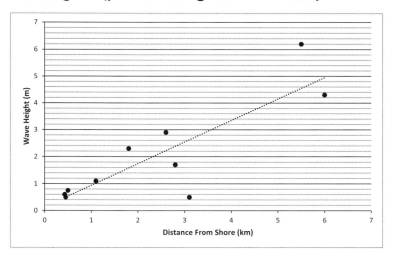

Figure 4.5 is a scatter plot of the buoy data in Table 4.4. One way of summarizing data in a scatter plot is to calculate an average relationship between the data points, which is called a *line of best fit*. This approach is used for data that are not *sequential, such as these*

buoy wind-speed data points. (Some examples of sequential data include time measurements and dates, such as if wind speed at one buoy were recorded over a period of time and then graphed.) In this plot, notice that, in general, the farther offshore the buoys are, the higher the wave heights are. Except with the outlier Buoy 6 data pair at (3.1, 0.5), there is a reasonably strong relationship between distance from shore and wave height. We describe it as "reasonably strong," because most of the values are reasonably close to the best-fit line. The outlier data pair was excluded in calculating this best-fit line.

Figure 4.6. Types of data scatter around lines of best fit

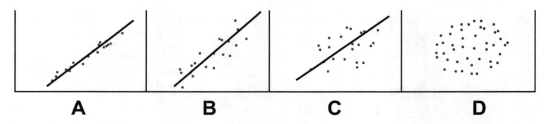

Source: Bowen and Bartley 2014.

We can better understand the strength of the relationship between these two variables by examining four common data-scatter patterns encountered in scatter plots (Figure 4.6). As the figure shows, they vary (from left to right) from following a pattern quite tightly to having more and more variation, until there is no obvious pattern. In these representations, data that follow the pattern in *A* have a very strong relationship, whereas those in *B* and *C* have a progressively weaker (although still present) relationship. A weak relationship might indicate that

- the outcome is being influenced by another variable not yet accounted for (given that an *x-y* graph only has two variables);

- controls were not effectively enacted; and/or

- there actually is *variation* in the variables being measured (often the case in biology).

The pattern in D is that of no pattern, which means there is no discernible relationship between the two variables on the *x-y* axes. Importantly, "no relationship" is still a research finding and you should still report it. Just to be clear: Not finding an expected relationship between variables is an acceptable research finding. One criticism of professional science is that it is difficult to get no-relationship papers published; however, students should be encouraged to write reports about their findings, even if they conclude that there is no pattern in their data.

Figure 4.7. Types of relationships between variables: Straight-line (A) and curved (B) and (C), which essentially are mirror images along the diagonal axis)

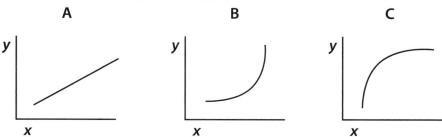

There are many types of relationships between two interval–ratio variables that might be apparent on scatter plots, but most are like the three examples in Figure 4.7 (or some combination of them, such as a sigmoid shape, which is a combination of [B] and [C]). The pattern in the scatter plot of our current data analysis (Figure 4.5, p. 55) is a straight-line relationship, as shown in Figure 4.7 (A), and is the relationship described using the model formula $y = mx + b$. Two types of curved relationships are also common in nature, as shown in Figure 4.7 (B) and (C). These curved relationships between the x and y variables should also be discussed in the conclusions of a study (as students often tend to reject a curvilinear relationship as "no relationship" and therefore not discuss it).

Another relationship sometimes shown in x-y scatter plots is a cycle (Figure 4.8). Scatter plots of cycles usually have an x-axis showing increasing time and usually do *not* show a best-fit line through the data points. Such graphs often join the data points together in the order they were collected, which makes sense because the events the data points represent are related (for example, what happens at 8:00 a.m. is related to what happened at 6:00 a.m., when the previous piece of data was collected). They show cycling of data over a period of time, and both the variation *around* the overall cycle pattern (and changes in that variation) and the cycling of the pattern over time contribute to the conclusions drawn. Using a scatter plot to graph cycles is common in some science disciplines. For example, in the atmospheric sciences, climatologists might track the mean daily temperature over many years at higher latitudes to investigate whether the seasonal cycle is changing over a long time period. If they were to find that the plot's peaks become higher and its valleys lower, that would indicate a greater shifting between extremes.

Figure 4.8. A cycling relationship over time

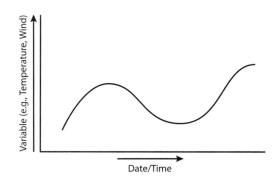

HOW SCIENTISTS COMMUNICATE ABOUT THEIR DATA

So far, we have entered the data into tables, created graphs to show patterns in the data, identified those patterns, and noted the strength of the patterns by looking at the data scatter. Now we will discuss how scientists talk—and write—about their findings. Scientists present their conclusions and ideas to the broader scientific community for evaluation by other scientists. Scientists use hedging language to communicate about their research, because scientific findings and claims are probabilistic in nature—they cannot be certain, but rather only are some degree of probable.

HEDGING LANGUAGE

Because scientific findings are probabilistic in nature, scientists use hedging language to indicate the level of certainty of their results or ideas. Here are some examples of hedging words and phrases:

- Seems, tends, looks like, appears to be, could be
- Is certain, is sure, believes, thinks, doubts
- Indicates, suggests, assumes
- Will, will not, must, can, cannot, would, could, might
- Often, frequently, usually, typically, sometimes, occasionally
- Certainly, definitely, clearly, probably, likely, possibly, perhaps, conceivably
- Certain, definite, clear, probable, possible
- Certainty, probability, likelihood, assumption, possibility

Traditionally, schools have taught students to make claims that are often quite absolute and deterministic. For example, students often make claims such as "A causes B" or "Dogs run faster than cats." Using deterministic language is problematic, because it can influence how much evidence people believe is necessary to make a claim. Instead, you should encourage your students to use hedging language that indicates how certain they are about their results. By doing so, you are encouraging them to be more scientific in their writing and helping them to develop a more probabilistic understanding of scientific claims. For instance, consider how these sentences have different meaning:

- Wind speed was higher closer to shore.

- Wind speed was usually higher closer to shore.

- Wind speed was often higher closer to shore.

- Wind speed was sometimes higher closer to shore.

Note that the first sentence makes wind speed sound as though it is *always* faster, and each subsequent sentence seems to indicate that wind speed being higher near the shore is less and less frequent.

EFFECT OF DETERMINISTIC LANGUAGE

The public often expects scientists to give definitive answers, and scientists are often reluctant to do so. Perhaps this expectation stems from people being taught to use deterministic, absolute language in schools when learning about science. Some researchers, including Mike, believe that teaching students to think about science deterministically places an unrealistic burden of proof on scientists that the scientists cannot meet. In addition, this deterministic baseline might influence politicians to want more proof than science can provide before they act. It is easy to see how this dynamic might cause problems.

In addition to helping students understand the probabilistic nature of science, teaching them to write about their conclusions using hedging language also teaches them that having perfect patterns among variables (that is, all data points being on the best-fit line) is not essential to be able to draw conclusions about and discuss implications of the results in science.

We also encourage you to be careful about allowing students to make statements indicating that the results of an investigation *prove* their hypothesis. Results can support or not support a hypothesis, but they cannot prove one. One of the fundamental principles of science is that all findings be falsifiable. Every investigation is fair game for repeating, and different results in a subsequent investigation could support a different conclusion. Make sure your students are using the language of science when they write about their results.

EXCEPTIONS TO THE GENERAL RULES FOR SUMMARIZING DATA

This section is applicable for some middle school science teachers and many high school science teachers, but probably is beyond what most elementary teachers will need in working with their students. It also involves a bit of math—so if you are not a "math person," you might decide to skip it (although we hope you will read it).

One of the common ways to summarize data and make it easier to understand is to calculate a mean (average) and use that mean in the data tables. This chapter's examples and tables have demonstrated the need in many instances to determine the mean of a large volume of real-time data to be able to easily discern patterns and trends in those data. Calculating arithmetic means—which show the "central tendency" or middle part of the value range— work for most variable types, but not for all types.

For some types of data, it is not scientifically correct to calculate an arithmetic mean, because the scales used to quantify the data are not linear. Some examples of these data types are logarithmic scales such as the pH, Richter scale, and decibel scale (sound), and empirical measures that produce ordinal data, such as the Beaufort scale for wind speed.

Log scales are multiples of a base. A simple logarithmic scale goes up 1, 2, 3, 4, 5, etc.; however, those sequential values actually represent 10, 100, 1,000, 10,000, 100,000, and so forth (see Table 4.5). For ordinal (ordered-category) data, the differences between values are not necessarily equal. For either of these, calculating an arithmetic mean will not produce correct and meaningful numbers.

Table 4.5. Logarithmic scale data

Log Value	Real Value
1	10
2	100
3	1,000
4	10,000
5	100,000

In many cases, the correct way to deal with these types of data is too complicated for middle school students and many high school students. In the interest of getting your students to understand the big picture, as a teacher, you might decide to have students calculate an arithmetic mean even though it is technically the incorrect approach. For example, Mike has had middle level students calculate an arithmetic mean of pH values (when students have done multiple samples); however, he has also told those students that arithmetic means are not the correct way to do it, but that the right way was too complex for them to learn at that time.

Consider this simple example of the problem, using Table 4.5. Imagine that you collected three data samples that were log-scaled: 1, 1, and 4. Their mean would be

$$(1 + 1 + 4)/3 = 6/3 = 2.$$

If you translated that mean log value of 2 into its "real" value, it would be 100; however, if you calculated the mean using the real values in the first place, you would get

$$(10 + 10 + 10{,}000)/3 = 10{,}020/3 = 3{,}340.$$

That would be the "correct" answer to the calculation, but 3,340 is very different from the 100 obtained by calculating the mean of the log value. Clearly, the amount of error in the results when calculating the means of logs is quite large, and that is why you cannot calculate a useful mean from pH, decibel-level, and Richter-scale values, and the other similar types of variables. Scientists want their assessment of variables' relationships to be as precise as possible, and so calculating means from logarithmic scale values is not considered acceptable scientific practice; however, as we noted earlier, as a teacher, you must decide whether that practice is an acceptable workaround for the interim by weighing what your students can do against what is correct practice and what you are trying to teach them. For example, in this example scenario, unless they had already learned about logarithms, Mike would instruct his middle school students to report a mean value of 2 because the logarithmic conversions would be too advanced for them.

It is also incorrect to calculate means of ordinal data. For example, assume the coffee shop in our earlier example named their coffee cup sizes 1, 2, and 3 instead of small, medium, and large. If they placed a supply order for three packages of size 2 cups, two packages of size 1, and four packages of size 3, then calculated the mean of those values, you would get 2.2. However, it would not make sense to say that the order was for a mean cup size 2.2, because a package of size 2.2 cups does not exist. In this instance, the correct "mean" for ordinal data is a median or "middle value"—and you would order the data as either

1, 1, 2, 2, 2, 3, 3, 3, 3

or

Small, Small, Medium, Medium, Medium, Large, Large, Large, Large

to represent the quantities and sizes of the cups, and then choose the middle value, which in this case is either "2" or "medium." So, the "mean" package is of "medium" cups.

There are many types of ordinal-level variables, including scales used to measure wind force (Beaufort wind force scale), tornado strength (Fujita-Pearson and Enhanced Fujita

Table 4.6. Summary of data variable types

Type of *x*-Axis Data Variable		Table Design	Typical Graph	Typical Analysis	Predictive Ability
Descriptive Name	Formal Name				
Category Data	Nominal Data			**Simple**: Heights of the bars (that is, means) are compared **Better**: Some consideration of "data scatter" (how the data are scattered around the means) is used to allow comparison of the means.	Not in most cases, because the variables in the columns are independent of each other.
Data are collected in categories that have no order, for example, comparing the mean running speeds of cats and dogs.					
Ordered Category Data	Ordinal Data			**Simple**: Differences between means are compared and overall pattern is examined. **Better**: The data scatter around the means is used for context to compare the means and the overall pattern.	Some predictive ability. Because the variables are in order, means for new variables that lie between old ones can be estimated to be between their means.
Data are collected in ordered categories, for example, comparing the time coffee takes to cool in small, medium, and large cups.					
Measured Data	Interval–Ratio Data			**Simple:** Data points are plotted and the general pattern described. **Better:** The line of best fit is drawn and the slope and "fit" of the line of best fit are described.	Good predictive ability. An unmeasured point on the *x*-axis can be chosen and a "response" (that is, a *y*-variable) can be estimated.
Data are collected as measurements for the *x*-axis, for example, examining the relationship between arm length and leg length (which gives *x–y* data pairs). The *x*-axis data may be a sequential variable, such as time or date information.					
var = variable					

Source: © G. Michael Bowen 2016. Used with permission.

scales), and hurricane strength (Saffir-Simpson Hurricane Wind Scale). So in this case, you have two ways of "averaging"; you could find the median of all the "categories" on the scale (as in the two examples above), or you could convert each "category""on the scale to the "middle" (median) wind speed of the range the category represents and, in that case, then calculate the mean of those median wind speeds in kilometers or miles per hour. Often, the method for this is to look up the scale values and the wind speeds associated with them (for example, online through the National Oceanic and Atmospheric Administration) and enter each median value of the wind-speed range into the table for calculating the mean. For example, a Beaufort wind force scale reading of 7 represents wind speed of 50 to 61 km/h. The median of this range—55 or 56, not the Beaufort number of 7—would be entered in the table for calculating a mean. If needed, that calculated mean wind speed can then be reconverted to the Beaufort number. Note that converting these ordinal scale values to real values, from which an arithmetic mean can be calculated, is far easier than converting logarithmic scale values to real values.

SUMMARY

Understanding different types of data helps students determine the best way to organize, graph, and analyze those data. The different types of data and their associated tables, graphs, and analysis notes covered in this chapter are summarized in Table 4.6.

When discussing data and their analysis, scientists usually use hedging language, because their findings are probabilistic. Nominal data are collected in categories that have no order and are organized in tables with each category as a column heading. Bar graphs typically are used to display nominal data. Nominal data typically are not predictive, because the data in each category are independent of one another. Ordinal data are collected in ordered categories (the categories have a direction) and are organized in tables that have each category as a column heading. Ordinal data categories are generally organized in a table from least to greatest or lowest to highest; this type of data is often displayed in a line graph and might provide some ability to predict values of new categories. Interval–ratio data are collected as measurements. Their data tables are organized as x-y pairs and graphed as scatter plots that, in many cases, have a line of best fit drawn on them and their slope described. When a best-fit line is not appropriate, the pattern (or cycle) of the data is described. Bowen and Bartley (2014) cover data analysis in much more detail, including statistical procedures.

REFERENCE

Bowen, G. M., and A. Bartley. 2014. *The basics of data literacy: Helping your students (and you!) make sense of data.* Arlington, VA: NSTA Press.

PART 2

SAMPLE
ACTIVITIES USING
REAL-TIME DATA

INTRODUCTION

This is the section you have been waiting for! Here, we provide sample activities for more than two dozen real-time investigations in your classroom. Each activity includes teacher notes that provide information for three-dimensional learning (disciplinary core ideas [DCIs], science and engineering practices, and crosscutting concepts), as well as background and technology information, an explanation of the data, and suggestions for scaling the lesson up or down.

Each activity also has a student handout that generally was developed at Level 1 or 2 of Tamir's Levels of Inquiry (see Table 3.1, p. 28). In most activities, both the problems and the procedures are given. Teachers who want to boost the level of inquiry might choose to forego the worksheet and initiate investigations that require greater student involvement in identifying problems and/or developing procedures. The data notes include information about the type of data, how to sample it, and what issues might need clarification. In addition, data enrichment exercises suggest other ways to explore the data.

The technology notes provide appropriate websites and apps (when available) from which to retrieve the data. We have attempted to use the most stable sources and to suggest multiple app options. Generally, websites for government agencies are stable for long periods—some, such as the National Oceanic and Atmospheric Administration (NOAA) and U.S. Geological Survey (USGS), have used the same internet domain for decades—however, over time, some URLs are likely to change. Should that occur with a resource provided in our activities, a web search often can provide the site's updated website link. Apps are much newer than internet domains in the world of technology; while you are using this book, newer, better apps might become available and some that we suggest here might be phased out. Again, a simple search through a browser can provide up-to-date resources.

Activities are grouped into chapters by the sphere of Earth they investigate: atmosphere, biosphere, geosphere, hydrosphere, and celestial sphere. These are tied directly to the DCIs that are connected to the *Next Generation Science Standards (NGSS)*. Although not every state has adopted or will adopt the *NGSS*, many of the DCIs are parallel to core ideas represented in state standards. The crosscutting concepts and science and engineering practices are not just integrated in *NGSS*, but are part of true three-dimensional learning as outlined in *A Framework for K–12 Science Education: Practices, Crosscutting Concepts, and Core Ideas* (NRC 2012). Although most of these investigations use multiple practices and concepts, we have narrowed the focus to one or two of each. We did this to emphasize the corresponding practices and concepts in the activities and analysis questions presented for students to address. For all websites, teachers should provide students with QR Codes for easy website access. Every activity provides links to the online sources it uses, and at the end of each chapter there is a table with the QR Codes for those online activity resources. If you are using a website not included in this text, you can easily make QR Codes for it. Just do an internet search for "QR Code generator" and several websites will appear in your search results that will allow you to generate your own QR Codes.

As you review these activities, you will see other ways to address the investigations and use the data. Good! We want these activities to be starting points for conducting real-time investigations, and hope we have given you the tools in the preceding chapters to develop inquiry activities that are well suited to your curriculum and students.

AVOIDING ASSUMPTIONS

Before we move on, there are two instructional implications that merit discussion. Having taught students at all levels from kindergarten through high school, Donna has some insights to share about working with big data that will make it easier for students to understand those data. The first one is that real-time data investigations can be used with students as young as third grade, depending on the investigation and the data. In some cases, the same data can be used at different levels for different purposes. At other times, you will need to filter the data or tailor the questions about a phenomenon to the level of your students. Regardless, let the purposes of your investigation drive your decisions about what data to use and how students should work with it.

Second, geography skills might also be an obstacle for your students when working with real-time data. Depending on the students, there might be significant gaps in their ability to locate events on a map and/or in their general understanding of the location where the data were produced. Although latitude and longitude are often introduced in elementary social studies, with mastery expected in middle school, many high school students struggle with this skill. Maps deal with information that is very abstract, for example, large distances; places students have never been; and information from within Earth, where even pictures provide little useful context.

MAPS AS ABSTRACTIONS

To help students deal with the abstract nature of maps, consider having them construct a to-scale map of a small local park or of the school grounds or even part of the school building. You will notice that in their maps, students leave blank areas, that is, areas with no content. You can engage students in talking about these blank areas, transition zones (outside), and other map-related issues. That conversation and problem solving, that is, the work of getting the map right, will give students understanding and context for thinking about and discussing maps they will use for activities in this book and elsewhere.

Whether you are discussing photoperiods at different latitudes; radiosonde data over Little Rock, Arkansas; ocean acidification in Grey's Reef; or plate tectonics off the coast of Australia, it helps to have a globe and a map handy. When possible, use local data. When you are not using local data, be sure to point out the location where data were generated and to discuss its relative location, using maps and a globe. Spend a minute reviewing how to find latitude and longitude on a map and choose a map projection that is easy for students to use. Sharing relevant news articles also engages your students and helps them see that the data they are using are current and are happening in real time and in real locations. This type of application integrates concepts across disciplines and engages students in authentic learning experiences.

USING GATHERED RESOURCES IN THE CLASSROOM

Data from government-funded research are public (in the public domain) and are not protected by copyright; however, you should always look for current content copyright policies on the relevant websites and apps. There are many resources for learning more about fair use for educational purposes. For example, Stanford University provides an online handbook on copyright for educational use (*http://fairuse.stanford.edu/overview/academic-and-educational-permissions*). Also, Cornell University provides an online checklist for conducting a fair-use analysis before using copyrighted materials (*http://copyright.cornell.edu/policies/docs/Fair_Use_Checklist.pdf*).

REFERENCES

Cornell University. Checklist for conducting a fair use analysis before using copyrighted materials. *http://copyright.cornell.edu/policies/docs/Fair_Use_Checklist.pdf*.

National Research Council (NRC). 2012. *A framework for K–12 science education: Practices, crosscutting concepts, and core ideas*. Washington, DC: National Academies Press.

Stanford University. 2016. Copyright and fair use: Academic and educational permissions. *http://fairuse.stanford.edu/overview/academic-and-educational-permissions*.

5

INVESTIGATIONS USING REAL-TIME ATMOSPHERE DATA

Real-time atmosphere data covers a broad range of phenomena, including weather, air quality, ozone, climate, and more. Weather data are collected by satellites, radar, ground-level instruments, and radiosondes (instruments attached to weather balloons that collect and transmit data about atmospheric conditions).

Real-time weather data are probably the most familiar. Long before "the internet" was a household term, weather data were reported in near real time in daily newspapers, on the radio, and on television news. Today, available weather data are much more comprehensive, and can easily be obtained for any city in any country, including past observations and predicted conditions. Public sources of atmospheric data include the National Oceanic and Atmospheric Administration (NOAA), the U.S. Environmental Protection Agency (EPA), NASA, and the National Weather Service (NWS). Other sources include the American Meteorological Society (AMS) and other nonprofit organizations, The Weather Channel, public and private colleges and universities, and private corporations.

Below, we share some of the most useful sources through which weather data that are accessible; in addition, Tables 5.1 and 5.2 (pp. 108 and 109, respectively) list all digital resources used in the chapter. Then, the rest of the chapter contains sample activities. You might want to use these activities as-is or modify them to fit your instructional purposes and students' ability levels. You might also find that our suggestions for using the data will trigger ideas for other investigations with those data.

The primary source of weather data is the NWS (*www.weather.gov*), whose website provides data for current conditions, including cloud cover, temperature, wind speed, wind direction, air pressure, and dew point. On their site, you will also find weather maps showing current conditions, locations of fronts, and predicted climate trends. In addition, past and predicted data are available there in multiple formats—text, charts, maps, tables, and graphs.

The NWS provides predictions in meteogram format (Figure 5.1, p. 72). Meteograms are a graphical model of weather and are used to analyze hourly data over a short period of time. One way to use a predictive meteogram is to have students use current weather maps to explain what factors might be influencing a forecast. For example, if students know that mid-latitude weather comes from the west, can they develop an argument that supports the predicted weather trends? Another possible activity would be for students to compare the weather outlook with actual weather data, and to assess whether temperatures rose and fell as expected, whether predicted precipitation arrived, and how accurate the outlook was.

Figure 5.1. National Weather Service meteogram for Des Moines, Iowa

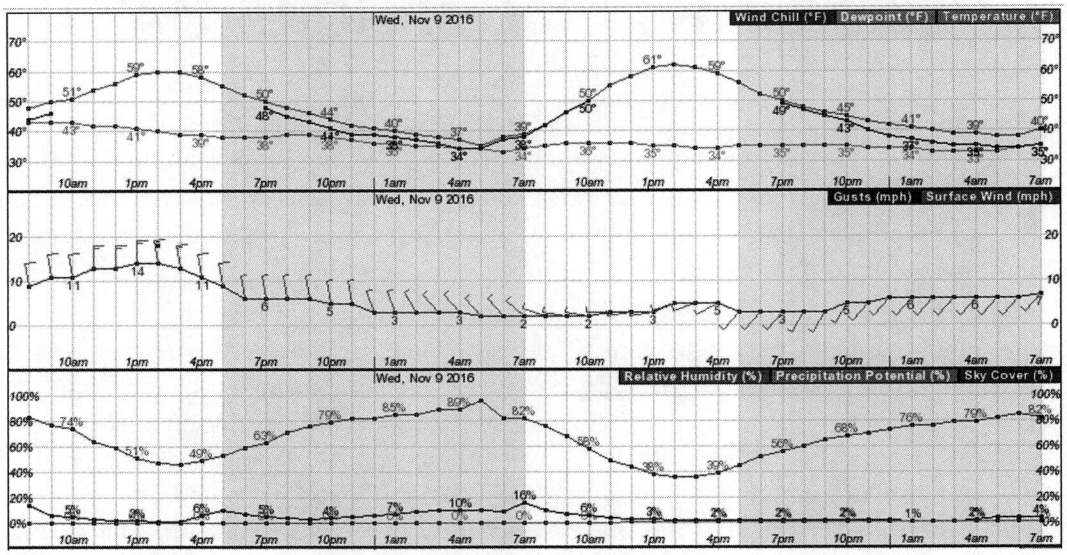

Source: http://forecast.weather.gov/MapClick.php?lat=41.57263&lon=-93.61571&unit=0&lg= english&FcstType=graphical

One of Donna's favorite websites for real-time weather data is *DataStreme* from the AMS (*www.ametsoc.org/amsedu/dstreme*). The *DataStreme* site was developed for use with a continuing education meteorology course for teachers, sponsored by the AMS. In addition to the meteorology course, they also have continuing education courses about oceans and about climate. The *DataStreme* site includes data provided for teachers enrolled in their course, but Donna has used it with middle and high school students. Their maps with surface data can be used to create isotherms or isobars (bands of equal temperature or equal pressure, respectively) and to explore wind patterns. Blank charts are available for students to create their own Stüve diagrams illustrating the vertical atmospheric temperature profile, or to create meteograms using NOAA data. In addition, educational materials are available from the *DataStreme* website and if you are interested, you might want to explore some of their continuing education courses for teachers.

If climate data are what you need, then NOAA is the most comprehensive source for long-term climate trends. One of its divisions, the National Climate Center (*www.climate.gov*), provides data on historical temperature, precipitation, drought, snow cover, carbon dioxide (CO_2) concentrations, solar energy output, and more. Using their *Global Climate Dashboard*

Figure 5.2. Screenshot from the NOAA Global Climate Dashboard

Source: www.climate.gov

(Figure 5.2), students can compare current data to overall trends and construct arguments that support or refute claims about the possible variables influencing climate change.

The NOAA *Environmental Visualization Laboratory* (*www.nnvl.noaa.gov*) is a rich source of atmospheric data for clouds, wind currents, stratospheric ozone, snow cover, and more, provided in graphic and animated formats. NOAA also provides real-time data on space weather (*www.swpc.noaa.gov*), which affects our atmosphere in multiple ways. For example, magnetic storms on the Sun interact with Earth's upper atmosphere to generate beautiful auroras, and long-term trends in the sunspot cycle have correlations with climate variations.

Air quality information is important in any environmental study of our atmosphere. The AIRNow website (*www.airnow.gov*) provides air-quality data hourly that includes tropospheric ozone and particulate matter ($PM_{2.5}$ and PM_{10}). The EPA website (*www.epa.gov/air-data*) provides daily concentrations of carbon monoxide (CO), nitrogen dioxide (NO_2), sulfur dioxide (SO_2), ozone (O_3), particulate matter (PM), and other pollutants. Student investigations can connect weather patterns to air quality, seasonal variations, and population, and can compare urban and rural areas. Want to know what the sources of air pollution are your area? The EPA website provides information about specific pollutants on their *Where You Live* page (*www3.epa.gov/air/emissions/where.htm*).

Webcams cannot be overlooked as a source of real-time data for weather. The NWS has webcams in many locations that students can use to correlate weather variables, such as cloud cover and air pressure data. Traffic, school, and other webcams can also help students to investigate weather trends, track local storm systems, and observe the effects of weather on the environment and the behaviors of people and animals.

REFERENCES

National Weather Service. *http://forecast.weather.gov/MapClick.php?lat=41.57263&lon=-93.61571&unit=0 &lg=english&FcstType=graphical.*

Climate.gov. *www.climate.gov.*

TEACHER NOTES: AIR QUALITY

Learning Goal	Students will explore the relationship between tropospheric ozone and temperature and how human populations affect ozone levels.
Disciplinary Core Ideas	• Weather and climate • Human impacts on Earth systems
Science and Engineering Practices	• Analyzing and interpreting data • Engaging in argument from evidence
Crosscutting Concepts	• Energy and matter: Flows, cycles, and conservation • Stability and change
Background Information	Tropospheric ozone is a gas that occurs naturally in the atmosphere in small amounts. It is also produced by photochemical reactions when sunlight interacts with pollutants such as nitrous oxides (NO_x), carbon monoxide (CO), and volatile organic compounds (VOCs) produced by automobiles, industry, and other human activities. High levels of ozone in the troposphere present a health risk to humans and other organisms. In people, respiratory problems are more likely to occur when ozone levels are elevated, which can be especially problematic for people with asthma. Because sunlight and heat increase ozone formation, ozone levels are often higher in summer than in winter. Also, because it is formed from pollutants such as CO, NO_x, and VOCs, ozone levels are usually higher in high-population areas than in rural areas.

DATA AND TECHNOLOGY

Online Sources	• AIRNow website (*www.airnow.gov*) for air-quality data • Weather Underground website (*www.wunderground.com/history*) for climate data • QR Codes: See Table 5.1 (p. 108).	AIRNow website screenshot
App and Device Sources	*Weather History Explorer* app for weather history data Device platforms: Android, iOS *AIRNow* app for air-quality data Device platforms: Android, iOS	*Source: www.airnow.gov.*

DATA AND TECHNOLOGY *(continued)*	
Technology Notes	Although there are dozens of apps that provide current air-quality data, the authors found no apps that provide historical data. The EPA *AIRNow* app provides current data. To find historical data, students should access the EPA AIRNow website through a browser on a computer or their device. This should not present much of a problem, because the data are easy to access through the website.
About the Data	**Data Sampling:** You might need to help students determine how to sample fairly. For instance, students might pick a particular day of the month to sample at a particular time or if there are multiple measures each day, they might calculate the mean (average) temperature for the day. **Data Type:** Temperature and ozone level are interval–ratio (measured) types of data. **Data Issues:** More-astute students might notice that the months being different lengths could cause minor data variation on the horizontal axis. One solution to this is to divide the number of days in a year by 12 and then measure at the same point in each of those periods. This will result in 12 evenly spaced measures; note they will be on different dates of each calendar month.
USING AND ADAPTING THE ACTIVITY	
About the Activity	Ozone levels are reported using an air quality index (AQI) that corresponds to actual ozone levels. The EPA AQI of 100 represents ozone levels of 0.075 parts per million (ppm) averaged over an 8-hour period. Levels of 0.070 ppm are considered the standard for EPA regulations. Students will need to understand that the method of data sampling will present outliers, because air quality is also affected by weather conditions such as wind, sky cover, and precipitation, which affect the availability of pollutants and/or the amount of sunlight available for photochemical reactions.
Scaling Down	Use a jigsaw activity by having students work in pairs, with each pair collecting one data point and sharing with the class. You can also use an app and track data over long periods of time, starting early in the year. Have students collect daily data and record it on a class weather calendar to correlate temperature and ozone only, without comparing it to less-populated areas. By the end of a full semester, the amount of data collected will be sufficient for analysis.

USING AND ADAPTING THE ACTIVITY *(continued)*	
Scaling Up	Have students collect other weather data, such as precipitation or wind speed. Then, they can compare data from sunny dates to data from rainy dates as an additional variable in producing photochemical ozone, or explore the role of wind in reducing pollutants. Students can also collect data related to population density for urban areas.
Extending	**Ozone Monitoring:** Students in urban areas can use ozone test strips to monitor ozone levels near their school. **Ozone Up High:** If it is the same molecule, why is ozone considered bad low in the atmosphere but good when up high in the atmosphere? Students can investigate stratospheric ozone using the NASA app *Earth Now,* and compare stratosphere and troposphere ozone levels. **Enrichment Using Data:** Have students construct a meteogram for temperature and ozone level (with the time variable on the horizontal axis) to examine variation over the year.

ASSESSMENT NOTES

Although ozone levels vary seasonally, they will be higher in the summer than at other times of the year because of increased ultraviolet light levels. Generally, trend lines should show a greater correlation between ozone and temperature in urban areas than in rural ones.

Name: _____

STUDENT HANDOUT: AIR QUALITY

Activity Goal	In this activity, you will explore the relationship between tropospheric ozone and temperature, as well as the effect of human activity on air quality.
Technology Notes	• Collect air-quality data from the EPA AIRNow website (*www.airnow.gov*). • Retrieve climate data from the *Weather History Explorer* app or the Weather Underground website (*www.wunderground.com/history*).
Orientation Questions	• Why are air-quality alerts more common in the summer than in the winter? • Why are urban areas (cities) more likely than rural areas to have air-quality alerts? • How do urban populations affect air quality?
Directions	1. From the list of monitored cities and states provided on the AIRNow website, choose a major city for which to collect data on ozone levels and temperature. In the data table, write that city beside the column heading "Urban Area." Groups should collect data from different locations. 2. From the same list of monitored cities and states, choose a rural area or a national park station that is geographically outside your chosen city. In the data table, write that location beside the column heading "Rural Area." You might have to look at locations in more than one state to find an acceptable location. 3. Using the Weather Underground website or the Weather History Explorer app, collect high-temperature data for both locations on the first Wednesday of every month for the past 12 months. Record the data in the data table, using °C or °F, as instructed by your teacher. 4. Using the AIRNow website, collect the ozone-level data for the same dates in both locations. 5. Complete the Data Analysis scatter plots for your data. 6. Complete the Analysis Questions, Conclusion, and Reflection Question sections.

DATA TABLE

Month	Urban Area:		Rural Area:	
	High Temperature (°_____)	Ozone Level	High Temperature (°_____)	Ozone Level
January				
February				
March				
April				
May				
June				
July				
August				
September				
October				
November				
December				

DATA ANALYSIS

To present your data, create a scatter plot showing results for each location, and then draw a best-fit trend line on each graph.

Urban area scatter plot

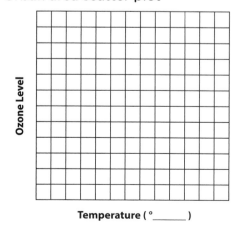

Rural area scatter plot

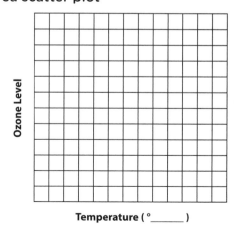

ANALYSIS QUESTIONS

1. What relationship is there between temperature and ozone level?

2. Based on what you understand about ozone production, how would you explain the outliers?

3. Describe the differences between an urban ecosystem and a rural ecosystem.

4. What difference, if any, did you note in the ozone-level data between the urban and rural areas?

5. Based on what you understand about ozone production, how would you explain the difference?

6. Compare your data to other groups. What similarities did you find in the data for urban and rural areas? What differences? How would you explain the differences?

CONCLUSIONS

Construct an argument based on the data you and your classmates collected, that explains the effects of human activity on air quality. Use examples from all of the data (yours and others') to support your claim. Describe how your understanding of energy and matter flow in a system is related to your findings.

REFLECTION QUESTIONS

1. Why is population density in urban areas a factor in tropospheric ozone production?

2. What is the role of seasonal solar energy input in tropospheric ozone production?

TEACHER NOTES: CLIMATE FROM POLE TO POLE

Learning Goal	Students will use mean (average) temperature data to determine changes in surface temperature over time in different areas of Earth.
Disciplinary Core Ideas	• Earth's systems • Weather and climate
Science and Engineering Practices	• Using mathematics and computational thinking • Engaging in argument from evidence
Crosscutting Concepts	• Cause and effect: Mechanism and explanation • Systems and system models
Background Information	The Goddard Institute for Space Science (GISS) Surface Temperature Analysis project (GISTEMP) monitors surface temperatures across the globe and publishes those data in a variety of ways. They offer access to over 135 years of data by month and region. In this activity, students will examine the mean surface temperature in three different regions of the globe—northern latitudes, middle latitudes, and southern latitudes. Students will explore the data set to determine differences in climate changes over time in these regions. Then, they will attempt to explain these differences, for example, decreased ice cover in the Arctic resulting in less sunlight being reflected and increased warming.

DATA AND TECHNOLOGY

Online Sources	• GISTEMP: *http://data.giss.nasa.gov/gistemp*. Under Table Data: Global and Hemispheric Monthly Means and Zonal Annual Means for the Land-Ocean Temperature Index, access the downloadable file *http://data.giss.nasa.gov/gistemp/tabledata_v3/ZonAnn.Ts+dSST.txt* • QR Codes: See Table 5.1 (p. 108).	GISTEMP Team, 2015 screenshot *Source: http://data.giss.nasa.gov/gistemp.*
App and Device Sources	No appropriate apps were located.	
Technology Notes	The GISTEMP website is not responsive in design, so students might find it a challenge to view on small devices. Students can explore multiple data sets on the website; however, this activity uses only the data set for zonal annual means, accessible at *http://data.giss.nasa.gov/gistemp/tabledata_v3/ZonAnn.Ts+dSST.txt*	

	DATA AND TECHNOLOGY (*continued*)
About the Data	**Data Sampling:** The GISTEMP project data set is very large, containing over 135 years' worth of data for multiple regions of Earth. If students do not have access to a graphing tool, you will need to help them select a sampling technique that will yield a manageable data set.
	Data Type: The data used in this activity are the interval–ratio (measured) data type, graphed in a scatter plot, with time in years on the *x*-axis. In this type of graph, the data are often joined point to point.
	Data Issues: Students might be confused by the temperature data displayed in the table. The data represent the amount above or below the mean global temperature, which is estimated to be 14°C (57°F), derived using temperature data for the years 1951 to 1980. The multiplier for the data is 0.01 and the unit is °C.
	Enrichment Using Data: Have students use the monthly northern and southern hemisphere data to determine whether there is a seasonal pattern for climate change.

	USING AND ADAPTING THE ACTIVITY
About the Activity	It might be helpful for students to have an understanding of global climate change. Students should have some idea that large bodies of water change temperature more slowly than land does. Use a jigsaw activity to help students more efficiently process data. Divide the class into initial groups of three. Assign each person in the initial groups a letter: A, B, or C. Now, have the students gather in different groups by letter to create graphs. Group A should graph the northern latitudes; Group B, the middle latitudes; and group C, the lower latitudes. When the graphs are completed, students return to their initial groups to compare graphs.
Scaling Down	Simplify this activity by using only the data for the Northern and Southern Hemispheres, instead of using data for the three latitude bands.
Scaling Up	Have students examine all eight latitude bands instead of just three. How might the differences in climate change in different regions affect ecosystems in those regions?
Extending	Have students conduct background research to explain the differences that they see in impacts of climate change across different latitude bands.

ASSESSMENT NOTES
Regardless of which data set is used, trends will show an increase in mean temperatures. The Southern Hemisphere will show less change than the Northern Hemisphere.

Name: _____   ATMOSPHERE

STUDENT HANDOUT: CLIMATE FROM POLE TO POLE

Activity Goal	In this activity, you will explore differences in climate change over time in different latitudes.
Technology Notes	Data for this activity will come from the Goddard Institute for Space Science (GISS) Surface Temperature Analysis (GISTEMP) at *http://data.giss.nasa.gov/gistemp*. The direct link to the data is *http://data.giss.nasa.gov/gistemp/tabledata_v3/ZonAnn.Ts+dSST.txt*.
Orientation Questions	• How have mean (average) temperatures changed over the past 120 years? • Are there differences in mean temperature changes in different latitudes?

Directions	Your teacher will assign you to an initial group and then to a graphing group that will look at data for a specific region of Earth. Your teacher also will help you determine how to sample your assigned data set.
	1. In your graphing group:
	   a. Graph the data for your region using a graphing tool or the graph provided.
	   b. Answer the Regional Analysis Questions for your region.
	2. Reconvene as your initial group. Each initial group will have at least one person from each region of Earth. In your initial group:
	   a. Answer the Global Analysis Questions by comparing the graphs from each region.
	   b. Complete the Conclusion and the Reflection sections.

DATA ANALYSIS

I am exploring the _____ region (for example, Northern Hemisphere [NHem], 24N to –24S).

Graph the mean temperature differences for your region:

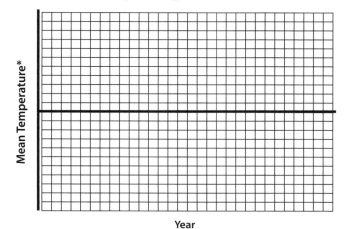

Year

*compared to the 1951–1980 global mean in the 0.01°C

REGIONAL ANALYSIS QUESTIONS

The temperatures you graphed in this activity are shown as the difference from the global mean of temperatures measured from 1951 to 1980 (that is, 14°C). The multiplier for the temperature differences in the data table is 0.01 and the unit is °C.

1. What was the mean temperature for your region in the following years?

    1880 _____   1947 _____   2015 _____

2. What general trend did you notice in your data?

GLOBAL ANALYSIS QUESTIONS

1. How did the general trend for your data compare with the trends in other regions?

2. How is the change in temperature different across different regions of Earth?

3. Describe the differences in geography (for example, amount of land versus the amount of water, quantity of ice cover) for the different regions represented in your group.

CONCLUSIONS

Use your answer to question 3 to explain the differences that you saw in question 2.

REFLECTION QUESTION

How does thinking about Earth as a system help you explain the differences that you found?

TEACHER NOTES: EXTREME WEATHER

Learning Goal	Students will use a National Oceanic and Atmospheric Administration (NOAA) database to identify extreme weather events throughout the United States in different locations or over time.
Disciplinary Core Ideas	• Earth's systems • Weather and climate
Science and Engineering Practices	• Analyzing and interpreting data • Using mathematics and computational thinking
Crosscutting Concepts	• Cause and effect: Mechanism and explanation • Patterns
Background Information	The NOAA *Storm Events Database* contains records of significant weather events that have occurred in the United States since 1950. Significant weather events include severe weather (dangerous meteorological phenomena that cause significant property damage, injury and/or death, and/or social and business disruption) and extreme weather (weather events extremely unusual for a given area, for example, snow in San Diego). NOAA attempts to format and standardize event data. Event data are recorded geographically by county and state.
DATA AND TECHNOLOGY	
Online Sources	• NOAA National Centers for Environmental Information *Storm Events Database* website: *www.ncdc.noaa.gov/stormevents*. • QR Code: See Table 5.1 (p. 108).
App and Device Sources	No appropriate apps were located for this activity.
Technology Notes	The *Storm Events Database* does not have a responsive design, so students might find it a challenging to view on small devices. Students can use the database to explore multiple types of events (for example, hail, tornado, heavy precipitation, dense fog, extreme heat or cold) nationwide, by state, or for a specific county within a state. Each event describes the date, location, magnitude, and damage (property, death, injury). The database search function only returns 500 data points per search, so students will need to pay attention to how they sample and collect data.

DATA AND TECHNOLOGY (*continued*)	
About the Data	**Data Sampling:** The NOAA *Storm Events Database* is huge. It contains tens of thousands of storm events that have occurred throughout the United States over more than 60 years. A variety of information is collected for each storm event. As a result, students will need to give careful consideration to how they constrain their data sampling.
	Data Type: The database contains all three types of data: Nominal, ordinal, and interval–ratio.
	Data Issues: Students might need to revise their sample size or conduct multiple searches to acquire the data they need to answer their investigation question. The NOAA *Storm Events Database* only displays 500 weather events for each search.

USING AND ADAPTING THE ACTIVITY	
About the Activity	• This activity is designed to allow students significant freedom in their exploration (Tamir, Level 3; see Table 3.1, p. 28). Students will be able to explore the data set, determine a question to guide their investigation, define the data sample to collect, and analyze their data.
	• Student investigations will focus on comparing weather events in different regions within the same time frame, or over time in the same region.
Scaling Down	Students who do not have experience creating their own investigation questions will need support in this activity. One possible support would be for students to generate questions individually or in small groups and then publicly share those questions with the class. Students could then use one of their own questions or select an interesting question shared by another student.
Scaling Up	The complexity of the activity can be increased by challenging students to look at larger samples of data.
Extending	**Enrichment Using Data:** The open-ended nature of this activity should provide plenty of opportunities for student enrichment.

SAMPLE INVESTIGATION QUESTIONS
The NOAA *Storm Events Database* provides an opportunity for students to craft many unique questions. The process described in the student handout will give them a sense of what is possible, but they may need support crafting and revising their question. A good question provides guidance for how students will sample data. Some sample questions are as follows: • Have the number of tornados per year in Oklahoma increased over the past 20 years? • Have the number of extreme heat days per year in Nevada increased over the past 50 years?

SAMPLE INVESTIGATION QUESTIONS *(continued)*
• Have the number of deaths from extreme heat in the United States increased or decreased over the past 30 years? • Over the past 20 years in Wisconsin, which month has experienced the most heavy-precipitation days (rain and/or snow)? • Over the past five years, which has caused more property damage, tornados, or floods? • Over the past five years, which county in Illinois has had the most floods? • Has there been an increase in heavy snow events in Massachusetts over the past 30 years?
ASSESSMENT NOTES
Because this activity is designed as an open-ended investigation, the data produced can vary widely. Assessment should be based on student interpretation of data and presentation of their research project.

Name: _____

STUDENT HANDOUT: EXTREME WEATHER

Activity Goal	In this activity, you will design an investigation to determine whether there are patterns in extreme weather events.
Technology Notes	The National Oceanic and Atmospheric Administration (NOAA) *Storm Events Database* contains information about extreme weather events in the United States since January 1950. Data can be accessed at *www.ncdc. noaa.gov/stormevents*.
Orientation Questions	What patterns (either location-based or over time) can you identify by using the NOAA *Storm Events Database*?
Directions	1. Begin by conducting a few searches using different criteria (location, type of weather, varying time ranges) to orient yourself to the type of data in the *Storm Events Database*. 2. Complete the Investigation section, based on data available in the database. In general, investigation questions will compare weather events in different locations within the same time period or compare weather events in one location over a long time period.

INVESTIGATION

1. After conducting a variety of searches, list the types of data that you could compare (for example, time of year versus heavy snow event, change in the number of extreme heat days over time). Include at least five possible comparisons.

2. Select the comparison you listed in question 1 that interests you the most. Think about how you will sample (select) data from the database for analysis. For example, if you are comparing weather events at two locations, what will the time period be? Or, if you are comparing changes in a weather event over time in one location, will you use data for 20 years, 30 years, or longer?

3. Write your investigation question. It should provide information about the location, weather event or other information, and the time period for the data sample that you will use.

4. Draw a data table to use to collect your data. Before collecting data, have your teacher approve your responses to questions 3 and 4.

5. Collect your data and display them in a graph.

6. From the data you collected, what claim (that is, what answer to your investigation question) can you make? How is this claim supported by evidence from your data? What might be the cause of the patterns that you found?

7. Create a poster that includes your investigation question, data table, graph(s), and conclusion.

TEACHER NOTES: WEATHER MAPPER

Learning Goal	Students will use weather data to create a current weather map by drawing station models for multiple locations.
Disciplinary Core Ideas	• Earth materials and systems • Weather and climate
Science and Engineering Practices	• Developing and using models • Engaging in argument from evidence
Crosscutting Concepts	• Cause and effect: Mechanism and explanation • Systems and system models

Background Information	Station models are used to show the current conditions on a weather map. They include symbols and data to show current temperature, dew point, air pressure, cloud cover, wind speed, and wind direction. A sample is shown to the right. These station models provide an overview of easy-to-read data that can be used not only to understand current conditions, but also to predict future conditions.	Sample weather station model

DATA AND TECHNOLOGY		
Online Sources	• National Weather Service (NWS) website: *www.weather.gov* • Weather Underground website: *www.wunderground.com* • QR Codes: See Table 5.1 (p. 108).	*NWS* website screenshot **Current conditions at Dodge City, Dodge City Regional Airport (KDDC)** Lat: 37.77°N Lon: -99.98°W Elev: 2592ft. Fair **74°F** 23°C Humidity 18% Wind Speed SW 12 mph Barometer 29.58 in (999.7 mb) Dewpoint 28°F (-2°C) Visibility 10.00 mi Last update 6 Mar 4:52 pm CST More Local Wx	3 Day History	Hourly Forecast *Source:* National Weather Service. *www.weather.gov.*
App and Device Sources		*Storm* app Device platform: iOS
		Weather Underground app Device platform: iOS, Android

DATA AND TECHNOLOGY (continued)	
Technology Notes	The NWS website has a responsive design and can be used easily on small devices. All data are presented in text form (see the website screenshot above). The *Storm* and *Weather Underground* apps show wind direction as pointers on a 360° compass to make it easier for students to identify wind direction. If you are using these apps, have the students open the app settings and change the units for air pressure from inches to millibars so that they will be using scientific units rather than U.S. customary ones.
About the Data	**Data Sampling:** No sampling problems anticipated. **Data Type:** Wind direction, wind speed, temperature, and air pressure are all the interval–ratio data type. **Data Issues:** No data issues anticipated.
USING AND ADAPTING THE ACTIVITY	
About the Activity	Before conducting this investigation, students should have an understanding how weather data are collected and what they mean. They should understand the difference between temperature and dew point. Students must also understand the difference between high and low air pressure, how air pressure is measured (millibars rather than inches). In addition, they should understand that air pressure data values omit the leading "9" or "10" and are extended to one decimal place.
Scaling Down	You can simplify this activity by having each student collect data from one location and contribute it to a class map for discussion and analysis, rather than producing individual maps.
Scaling Up	Make this investigation more complex by increasing the number of locations for which models are provided so that there is one model per state. Another option to increase complexity is to have students draw either isobars or isotherms on their maps based on the data collected.
Extending	**Weather Channel News:** Students can use the maps they create to produce weather report videos explaining the current weather conditions around the country and in specific cities. **Go International!:** Students can collect and analyze data for locations worldwide using the website *http://weather.org*. **Station Model Journals:** Have students keep a station model journal for the weather in a specific location for a week. Then they can describe the changes that occur over time.

USING AND ADAPTING THE ACTIVITY (*continued*)	
Extending (*continued*)	**Enrichment Using Data:** Have students use the station models to identify areas of high pressure and low pressure, predict a weather track (that is, how those highs and lows will move), and then create station models on subsequent days along the tracks to observe the changes.

ASSESSMENT NOTES
In general, low pressure is associated with cloudy skies and high pressure with clear skies. Students should see patterns emerge, such as counterclockwise winds around areas of low pressure or clockwise winds around areas of high pressure, and should be able to answer questions about current weather in specific locations based on data collected.

Name: _____

STUDENT HANDOUT: WEATHER MAPPER

Activity Goal	In this activity, you will construct a weather map with station models to show current weather conditions around the country.
Technology Notes	• Data for this activity will come from the National Weather Service website: *www.weather.gov*. • Your teacher might instruct you to use an app instead.
Orientation Questions	• How are weather maps produced? • What information is included on a weather map?
Directions	1. Collect weather data for 25 cities from the website or with an app. Try to spread your locations around the country so that your data are spread out on the map. 2. Construct a station model for each location on the map. 3. Draw a large *L* on the location with the lowest air pressure and an *H* on the location with the highest air pressure. 4. Complete the Analysis Questions, Conclusions, and Reflection Question sections.	Sample weather station model Temperature **74** Air Pressure **983** Current Conditions •• **72** Wind Speed and Direction Dewpoint Cloud Cover

ANALYSIS QUESTIONS

1. What patterns do you notice when comparing locations with different air pressures (lowest versus highest) and amounts of cloud cover (cloudy versus sunny)?

2. Do winds move clockwise or counterclockwise around areas of low pressure?

3. How do winds move around areas of high pressure?

4. When the temperature and dew point are the same or very close, precipitation is likely. According to the data you collected, where was it most likely to be raining or snowing? Was that precipitation rain or snow? How do you know?

5. What evidence does your map show that supports a cause-and-effect relationship between air pressure and cloudy weather?

CONCLUSIONS

Predict how you think the weather where you live will change over the next day or so. Use what you know about weather and evidence from your weather map to support your claim.

REFLECTION QUESTION

What advantage does the station model presentation have over a text presentation in showing weather data?

ATMOSPHERE

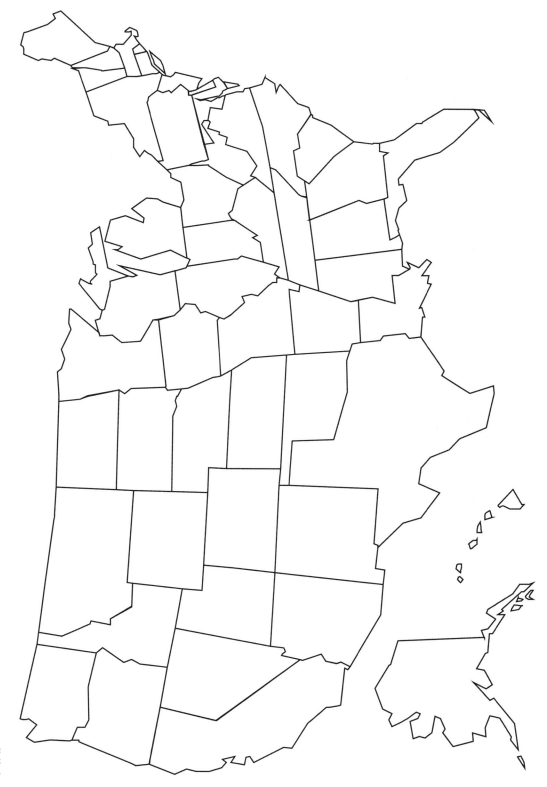

MAP

TEACHER NOTES: WEATHER STORIES

Learning Goal	Students will develop and analyze meteograms for select cities to construct a 24-hour history for a specific location.
Disciplinary Core Ideas	• Earth materials and systems • Weather and climate
Science and Engineering Practices	• Developing and using models • Constructing explanations and designing solutions
Crosscutting Concepts	• Systems and system models • Stability and change
Background Information	Meteograms are graphical models of weather data produced for a single location over a 24-hour period. Although there might be some variation in how meteograms are produced, they usually present temperature, dew point, wind speed, wind direction, precipitation, and air pressure data. Wind speed and wind direction can be shown using numeric data (knots and azimuth) or a station model symbol (✎). The data are graphed from left to right in order of oldest to most recent. The models show changes in conditions and can reveal the effects of storms and fronts.

DATA AND TECHNOLOGY

Online Sources	• National Weather Service (NWS) website: *www.weather.gov* • QR Code: See Table 5.1 (p. 108).	*NWS* website screenshot Current conditions at **Gainesville, Gainesville Regional Airport (KGNV)** Lat: 29.69°N Lon: 82.29°W Elev: 151ft. Fair **85°F** 29°C Humidity 39% Wind Speed E 5 mph Barometer 30.03 in (1016.6 mb) Dewpoint 57°F (14°C) Visibility 10.00 mi Heat Index 84°F (29°C) Last update 31 Oct 3:53 pm EDT Extended Forecast for Gainesville Regional Airport FL *Source:* National Weather Service. *www.weather.gov.*
App and Device Sources	**WU** WEATHER UNDERGROUND	*Weather Underground* app Device platform: iOS, Android
		Weather Mate app Device platform: iOS
Technology Notes	On the NWS website, you must select the "3 Day History" of a city to see data from the past. In the iOS-based app *Weather Mate*, you can see hourly data by choosing "Weather History" in the top menu bar and then selecting the date. The Android-based *Weather Underground* app displays the past several days of all relevant data except for air pressure.	

 NATIONAL SCIENCE TEACHERS ASSOCIATION

DATA AND TECHNOLOGY *(continued)*	
About the Data	**Data Sampling:** Teachers need to help students determine geographic location and day for which they will collect their data.
	Data Type: Temperature (often in °F), dew point (°F), wind speed (mph), precipitation (in.), and air pressure (millibars) are all the interval–ratio (measured) data type, and in a meteogram these are graphed against time (on the horizontal axis, another interval–ratio variable type), which is "sequential." Temperature, dew point, and air pressure are shown as a line graph. Wind speed, cloud cover, and wind direction are shown using symbols (wind barbs) and precipitation is shown using symbols representing the precipitation type.
	Data Issues: The value of the *y*-axis is determined individually for each data set, depending on the range of the data.
USING AND ADAPTING THE ACTIVITY	
About the Activity	This activity is most appropriately used at the end of a weather study unit because students should understand weather variables and know how to draw a station model. This is a two-part activity. First, students create a meteogram for a specific location using 24-hour data, and then they describe the changes that have occurred during that period. A very effective way to use this activity is to select cities where specific weather events have occurred during the past 24 hours. This allows students to see the effects from passage of cold fronts, land and sea breezes, storms, and more.
Scaling Down	Instead of having students create their own meteograms, have them locate and collect meteograms for specific cities from the *DataStreme* website (*www.ametsoc.org/amsedu/dstreme/metgram.html*). Then, have students construct explanations of how weather has changed in these locations. Teachers should provide sample meteograms that illustrate specific weather phenomena, such as the passing of a front.
Scaling Up	Ask students to identify cities in which a weather event has occurred over the past 24 hours and produce a meteogram to show the event. After they have interpreted their own data, students can trade meteograms with each other for interpretation. They should compare their explanations and construct arguments to defend their interpretations. In addition, students can compare meteograms for different cities experiencing the same phenomenon to see how different locations experience the same event.

USING AND ADAPTING THE ACTIVITY (*continued*)	
Extending	**Comparing Cities:** Comparing data from different cities experiencing the same event could be useful to help students see changes that occur as a result of weather systems. **Personalized Meteograms:** Students can construct personalized meteograms with data they collect themselves over a period of hours or days. **Enrichment Using Data:** In addition to the data already discussed, some meteograms could include humidity and visibility data.
ASSESSMENT NOTES	
For passage of a cold front through a specific location, students should note that the air pressure drops and then rises again when the front has moved through. Winds will shift from out of the south and east ahead of a front to out of the west and north behind it. Temperatures will drop and skies will often begin to clear after front has passed.	

Name: _____

STUDENT HANDOUT: WEATHER STORIES

Activity Goal	In this investigation, you will construct a meteogram from weather data and then construct an explanation for the changes that occurred during the period analyzed.
Technology Notes	For this activity, you will collect data from the National Weather Service (NWS) website at *www.weather.gov* or from a weather app suggested by your teacher.
Orientation Questions	How do local weather conditions change when a weather event occurs? What relationships between air pressure, temperature, and wind speed and wind direction can be observed as the weather conditions change?

Directions	Identify a city in which, a specific weather event has occurred in the past 24 hours (for example, a storm, the passage of a cold front, or another event). Your teacher will direct you on whether to collect those data for a specific city or for a city of your own choosing.
	
	 1. Gather hourly data for that city for the past 24 hours from the *NWS* website.
	
	 2. Construct and explain the meteogram.
	     a. Graph the data for temperature, dew point, wind direction, wind speed, precipitation, and air pressure into the meteogram on the reverse side of this handout. You will need to set your own scale for temperature and pressure based on the data you have collected. Use line graphs for temperature, dew point, and air pressure. Use station models to show wind speed and wind direction. Use raindrops and snowflakes to show precipitation: one for light precipitation, two for moderate, and three for heavy. Use the equal sign (=) to indicate fog.
	     b. Construct an explanation of the changes observed during the past 24 hours.
	
	 3. Complete the Analysis Questions, Conclusions, and Reflection Question sections.

Wind Direction
Wind barb shows direction wind is coming FROM

Flags show wind speed
Each full flag is 10 knots
(1½ flags = 15 knots)

Circle shows cloud cover

BLANK METEOGRAM

Temperature / Dew Point

Most Recent Data ——→

Winds and Sky Coverage

Precipitation

Air Pressure

After completing your meteogram, construct an explanation of the changes observed during the past 24 hours.

ANALYSIS QUESTIONS

1. What weather event were you collecting data for?

2. What changes did you note in the weather for the period over which this location experienced the weather event?

3. Were there any changes in one variable that seemed to correspond to changes in another variable? For example, did rising and falling of air pressure correspond to wind direction or sky cover?

4. How does a meteogram provide a record of meteorological changes that occur over time for a given location?

CONCLUSIONS

Compare your data and results with those of other students who explored the same or a similar event in other locations. What conclusions can you draw about how this type of weather event affects local conditions?

REFLECTION QUESTION

How might the data you analyzed in this activity help with prediction of changes during future weather events?

TEACHER NOTES: WIND BENEATH OUR WINGS

Learning Goal	Students will use flight take-off and landing patterns to better understand wind.
Disciplinary Core Ideas	• Earth materials and systems • Weather and climate
Science and Engineering Practices	• Developing and using models • Engaging in argument from evidence
Crosscutting Concepts	• Cause and effect: Mechanism and explanation • Patterns
Background Information	Wind direction affects how airplanes take off and land. Generally, aircraft will take off into the wind, because that has the effect of increasing the speed at which the wind passes over the wings. A strong headwind when landing provides resistance and helps slow the aircraft for a smoother landing. Although taking off and landing into the wind is preferable, the orientation of the airport landing strips influences the direction of landing. For example, larger airports often primarily use east–west landing strips, because north–south landing strips are not long enough for larger aircraft. Generally, knowing the direction flights take off and land can provide information about wind direction. This, in turn, can provide the location of high- and low-pressure systems. If you face the wind, low pressure will be to the right and high pressure to the left.

DATA AND TECHNOLOGY

Online Sources	• FlightAware website: *https://flightaware.com/live* • Weather Underground website for wind-direction data: *www.wunderground.com* • QR Codes: See Table 5.1 (p. 108).	FlightAware website screenshot
App and Device Sources	*FlightAware* app for flight data Device platforms: iOS, Android	
	Weather Underground app for wind data Device platform: iOS, Android	*Source:* FlightAware. *https://flightaware.com/live.*

DATA AND TECHNOLOGY *(continued)*	
Technology Notes	The FlightAware website and app allow students to see flight traffic in real time. There are usually so many flights that, to see individual aircraft, you must zoom in. Students should look for the major airports (indicated by white lines) designated in the activity, and identify planes landing or taking off by clicking on the airplane graphic. To find wind information, students can use many different websites and apps; however, the Weather Underground website and app allow students to view the information in map form.
About the Data	**Data Sampling:** No sampling issues are anticipated. **Data Type:** Wind speed is an interval–ratio type of data. Wind direction is often recorded as a cardinal direction (for example, north, south) or an intercardinal direction (for example, northwest, southwest), but these wind directions might also be recorded in compass degrees. **Data Issues:** Students might be familiar with only the coarser-grain cardinal and intercardinal directions and not with the finer-grain secondary-intercardinal directions (for example, south–southwest, west–southwest).
USING AND ADAPTING THE ACTIVITY	
About the Activity	In this activity, students will make inferences about wind direction and the location of high- and low-pressure systems from the landing and take-off patterns at various airports. Before participating in this activity, students should understand that winds blow clockwise around high-pressure systems and counter-clockwise around low-pressure systems in the Northern Hemisphere. Teachers might want to discuss how aircraft use the wind to assist in take-off and landing by flying into the wind when possible.
Scaling Down	Have students complete the investigation using landing and take-off paths to determine wind direction, without making conclusions about the location of high- and low-pressure systems.
Scaling Up	Have students predict the location of high- and low-pressure systems without verifying the wind direction for each airport. Airport runways are identified using numeric designations based on their compass setting (for example, runway 23 is at 230 degrees, runway 09 is 90 degrees). Students can find the designation for each runway at the airports shown to determine how it might affect flight take-off and landing.

	USING AND ADAPTING THE ACTIVITY (*continued*)
Extending	**Comparing Aircraft Speed:** Have students use the FlightAware website or app to find pairs of eastbound–westbound aircraft that are close in proximity. Ask students to compare the aircraft speed of the two aircraft and construct an explanation about why there is a significant difference. Additional information provided for each flight provides a rich source of data for students to analyze, for example, by calculating flight times, altitude, and airport traffic. **Enrichment Using Data:** Have students convert the cardinal directions to polar measure (degrees) so they can calculate the "degrees incorrect" of their predictions. These could also have a +ve or –ve component (that is, over or under the actual, respectively).

ASSESSMENT NOTES

There will not always be an observable pattern tied to current high- and low-pressure systems because airports generally only have two runways, often running generally east–west and north–south. Smaller airports might only have one. For this reason, expect some variation in the data and discuss reasons for the outliers with students.

Name: _____

STUDENT HANDOUT: WIND BENEATH OUR WINGS

Activity Goal	In this activity, you will use the flight patterns of aircraft to gather information about current weather conditions and to predict the locations of pressure systems. Pilots take off and land into the wind to use wind speed to their advantage. By observing aircraft landing and taking off patterns, you can make inferences about wind direction. Wind direction will tell you the approximate location of high- and low-pressure systems.
Technology Notes	To find flight data, use the *FlightAware* app or website (*https:// flightaware.com/live*). Wind-direction data can be obtained from the *Weather Underground* app or website (*www.wunderground.com*).
Orientation Questions	• What inferences can you make about wind direction based on the take-off and landing patterns of aircraft? • What information does wind direction provide about the location of high- and low-pressure systems?
Directions	**Part 1—Data Table** 1. For each airport in the data table, identify one aircraft approaching or departing the airport. Click on the plane to verify its flight path. 2. Record the flight information and direction in which the plane is moving in the data table. 3. Find two additional cities of your choosing and do the same. 4. Based on the direction at which each plane is landing, predict the direction from which the wind is blowing. Record your prediction in the data table. 5. Using the Weather Underground website link or app, locate each city. Record in the data table the direction from which the wind is actually blowing. **Part 2—Map** 6. Indicate the wind direction at each location on the map. 7. Once you know the wind direction at all of the airports, predict the location of high-pressure and low-pressure areas in the continental United States. Indicate your predictions on the map. 8. Go back to the Weather Underground website or app and select "Current Conditions" map. Compare the predicted locations of high- and low-pressure areas on your map to those on the website or app. 9. Complete the Analysis Questions, Conclusions, and Reflection Question sections.

DATA TABLE

Airport	City, State	Flight Number	Plane Direction	Predicted Winds	Actual Winds
ATL	Atlanta, Georgia				
DFW	Dallas–Fort Worth, Texas				
PHX	Phoenix, Arizona				
SLC	Salt Lake City, Utah				
ORD	Chicago, Illinois				
DCA	Washington, District of Columbia				
BOS	Boston, Massachusetts				
MSP	Minneapolis, Minnesota				

MAP

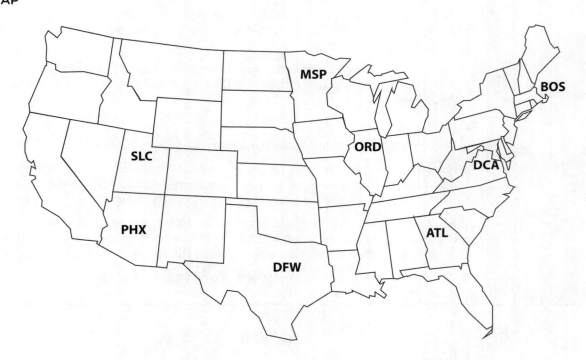

ANALYSIS QUESTIONS

1. How accurately were you able to predict wind direction from aircraft landing and take-off patterns?

2. What explanation can you give to explain why some predictions were not accurate?

3. How accurately were you able to predict the locations of pressure systems?

4. How do air traffic controllers use weather data to regulate aircraft landing and take-off patterns?

5. How would airports near the coast need to adjust landing and take-off patterns based on summer land and sea breezes?

CONCLUSIONS

Construct an argument that explains the relationship between aircraft take-off and landing patterns and wind direction.

REFLECTION QUESTION

Is the relationship between take-off and landing patterns coincidental or cause-and-effect? Explain.

Table 5.1. Data sources for atmosphere and climate investigations

Activity	Website	URL	QR Code
Air Quality	AIRNow	*www.airnow.gov*	
Climate From Pole to Pole	GISS Surface Temperature Analysis	*http://data.giss.nasa.gov/gistemp*	
Extreme Weather	NOAA *Storm Events Database*	*www.ncdc.noaa.gov/stormevents*	
Weather Mapper	National Weather Service	*www.weather.gov*	
	Weather Underground	*www.wunderground.com*	
Weather Stories	National Weather Service	*www.weather.gov*	
Wind Beneath Our Wings	FlightAware Flight Tracking	*https://flightaware.com/live*	
	Weather Underground	*www.wunderground.com*	

Table 5.2. Additional atmospheric and climate data sources

Website	URL	QR Code
American Meteorology Society	www.ametsoc.org/ams	
DataStreme	www.ametsoc.org/amsedu/dstreme	
EPA *Air Quality*	www.epa.gov/air-data	
NASA *Earth Observations*	http://neo.sci.gsfc.nasa.gov	
National Snow and Ice Data Center	http://nsidc.org	
NASA *Global Sulfur Dioxide Monitoring*	http://so2.gsfc.nasa.gov	
NOAA National Climate Center	www.climate.gov	
Air Quality—NOAA *Earth System Research Laboratory* Global Monitoring Division	www.esrl.noaa.gov/gmd	
NOAA *Environmental Visualization Laboratory*	www.nnvl.noaa.gov	

Table 5.2. (*continued*)

Website	URL	QR Code
NOAA *Climate Data Online*	*www.ncdc.noaa.gov/cdo-web*	
University of Wyoming Department of Atmospheric Science	*http://weather.uwyo.edu/upperair/sounding.html*	

6

INVESTIGATIONS USING
REAL-TIME BIOSPHERE DATA

The biosphere is the part of Earth that is composed of living organisms. This includes humans, ducks, grass, trees, snails, algae ... well, you get it. Data on animals, insects, and other life forms are often collected by researchers studying their behavior. Environmental scientists study the environment and how organisms interact with it. Information about people is often collected by governments and population researchers. Data can be collected using digital instruments, cameras, surveys, and even simply by observation.

Human populations—a topic in every environmental science course—can be explored in great detail at the U.S. Census Bureau website (*www.census.gov/topics/population.html*). Interactive maps are one way that population trends can be explored with real-time data. The *NASA Earth Observations (NEO)* website (*http://neo.sci.gsfc.nasa.gov*) provides real-time data for several Earth systems. The data sets in the site's "Life" category are graphic models—monthly maps that provide information about net primary productivity, leaf area, chlorophyll concentration, and several other research topics. The National Oceanic and Atmospheric Administration (NOAA) *Integrated Ocean Observing System Animal Telemetry Network (IOOS ATN)* website (*http://oceanview.pfeg.noaa.gov/ATN*) allows tracking of marine animals. Web cameras at zoos, nature conservatories, and other locations can provide a way for students to do population studies or watch interactions between organisms and their ecosystems. There are osprey cams, bee cams, fall-foliage cams, and even naked mole rat cams. These provide a rich source of data that help students to better understand how specific species function in their environment.

One useful investigation through which to explore how life interacts with the environment would be to correlate current sea-surface temperature to past and present movement of marine animals using the *IOOS ATN* website. Figure 6.1 (p. 112) contains screenshots of site content showing the movement of a tagged salmon shark over a six-month period in 2015. On the site, students can watch the movement of specific marine animals over a number of days or compare the most recent location of different species. Students also can use site information to infer the preferred conditions of different species and compare their inferences to information learned through environmental studies research.

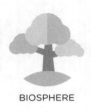

Figure 6.1. Sample of data available on the NOAA *Animal Telemetry Network* website

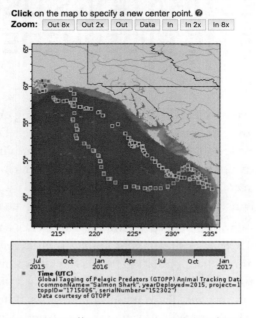

Source: http://oceanview.pfeg.noaa.gov/ATN.

Land use is a topic studied in every environmental science course. The U.S. Department of Agriculture (USDA) website (*www.nrcs.usda.gov*) provides data on land use and soil resources. A possible investigation using the *USDA* data would be to compare and contrast land-use trends for different states. For example, Figure 6.2 shows the latest data for land use for Montana and New Jersey. These two states are very different in many ways, including geography and population density. New Jersey has a population density of 1,210 people per square mile, whereas Montana's population density is seven people per square mile. You could ask students to investigate how land use in these states has changed over time, and to develop an explanation about why there are so many differences in land use in these states. How do weather and climate affect each's use of land? What other variables contribute to the differences shown?

Again, the investigations that follow are only a few of the many ideas that you could use to explore the biosphere. Use these as a starting point … and see what new ideas you generate with the real-time resources that are available. Tables 6.1 and 6.2 (pp. 138 and 139, respectively), list all digital resources used in this chapter.

Figure 6.2. Land-use comparison charts for Montana and New Jersey

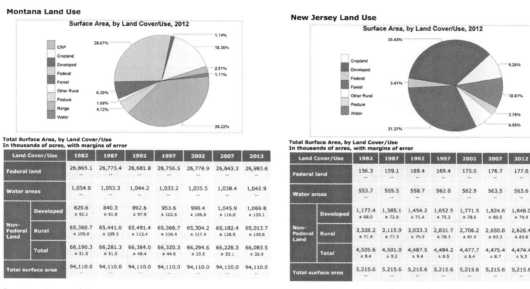

Montana Land Use

Total Surface Area, by Land Cover/Use
In thousands of acres, with margins of error

Land Cover/Use		1982	1987	1992	1997	2002	2007	2012
Federal land		26,865.1 --	26,775.4 --	26,681.8 --	26,756.5 --	26,779.9 --	26,843.3 --	26,983.6 --
Water areas		1,054.6 --	1,053.3 --	1,044.2 --	1,033.2 --	1,035.5 --	1,038.4 --	1,042.9 --
Non-Federal Land	Developed	829.6 ± 92.1	840.3 ± 91.9	892.6 ± 97.9	953.6 ± 102.6	990.4 ± 106.6	1,045.9 ± 116.0	1,069.8 ± 120.1
	Rural	65,360.7 ± 105.0	65,441.0 ± 105.3	65,491.4 ± 113.4	65,366.7 ± 116.4	65,304.2 ± 117.4	65,182.4 ± 126.5	65,013.7 ± 130.6
	Total	66,190.3 ± 51.5	66,281.3 ± 51.5	66,384.0 ± 48.4	66,320.3 ± 44.8	66,294.6 ± 33.5	66,228.3 ± 33.1	66,083.5 ± 32.9
Total surface area		94,110.0 --	94,110.0 --	94,110.0 --	94,110.0 --	94,110.0 --	94,110.0 --	94,110.0 --

New Jersey Land Use

Total Surface Area, by Land Cover/Use
In thousands of acres, with margins of error

Land Cover/Use		1982	1987	1992	1997	2002	2007	2012
Federal land		156.3 --	159.1 --	169.4 --	169.4 --	175.0 --	176.7 --	177.6 --
Water areas		553.7 --	555.5 --	558.7 --	562.0 --	562.9 --	563.5 --	563.6 --
Non-Federal Land	Developed	1,177.4 ± 68.0	1,385.1 ± 72.8	1,454.2 ± 71.4	1,652.5 ± 75.2	1,771.5 ± 78.6	1,824.6 ± 80.0	1,848.0 ± 79.9
	Rural	3,328.2 ± 71.4	3,115.9 ± 77.3	3,033.3 ± 75.5	2,831.7 ± 78.3	2,706.2 ± 81.9	2,650.8 ± 83.3	2,626.4 ± 83.6
	Total	4,505.6 ± 9.4	4,501.0 ± 9.2	4,487.5 ± 9.4	4,484.2 ± 8.5	4,477.7 ± 8.4	4,475.4 ± 8.7	4,474.4 ± 9.3
Total surface area		5,215.6 --	5,215.6 --	5,215.6 --	5,215.6 --	5,215.6 --	5,215.6 --	5,215.6 --

Source: Natural Resources Conservation Service. *www.nrcs.usda.gov/wps/portal/nrcs/rca/national/technical/nra/rca/ida.*

REFERENCES

Annenberg LLC. 2016. Explore. *http://explore.org.*

Natural Resources Conservation Service. *www.nrcs.usda.gov/wps/portal/nrcs/rca/national/technical/nra/rca/ida.*

TEACHER NOTES: ANIMAL BEHAVIOR ETHOGRAMS

Learning Goal	To understand the range and frequency of behaviors in which animals can engage, and how those might be affected by factors such as weather conditions or time.
Disciplinary Core Ideas	• Natural resources • Biogeology
Science and Engineering Practice	Obtaining, evaluating, and communicating information
Crosscutting Concepts	• Systems and system models • Energy and matter: Flows, cycles, and conservation
Background Information	Understanding issues of environmental science involves understanding how animals behave in their environmental settings and how abiotic features (for example, temperature, rainfall, wind, light, and humidity) might influence those behaviors. Scientists often construct behavioral descriptions (called ethograms) in relation to abiotic features to understand any links between those features and exhibited behaviors of the animals. There are many private, government, and university websites that show live video of animals "behaving" in their environment that could be used to help students understand the relationship between abiotic factors and the animals in a video.

DATA AND TECHNOLOGY		
Online Sources	• Explore: *http://explore.org*. Click on the "Live Cams" link. • QR Code: See Table 6.1 (p. 138).	Explore website screenshot *Source: http://explore.org.*
App and Device Sources	SAN DIEGO ZOO	*San Diego Zoo* app Platforms: iOS, Android
Technology Notes	The Explore website does not have a responsive design. Although students may be able to view the website information on their devices, this activity might work best on a full-size screen. The *San Diego Zoo* app is an alternative resource for animal cams and can be used on student devices for this investigation. Note that animals may or may not be visible at a specific time; therefore, it is better to have students conduct this activity on their own time (for example, at lunch, after school, at home, on weekends) so they can check back at different times to see how the animals are behaving.		

DATA AND TECHNOLOGY (*continued*)	
About the Data	**Data Sampling:** The complexity of data sampling depends on how active the animal is and whether the site shows one or two animals (for example, birds sitting on a nest) or many animals (for example, a herd at a watering hole in Africa). **Data Type:** If behavior frequencies are recorded over several days (or other periods of time), they would be interval-ratio data (but represented in a bar graph with time on the *x*-axis). **Data Issues:** Students are engaging in counts and lists of behavior to determine frequency and other data. If the counts occur at the same time each day, a bar graph can be used to compare data for the different days—clustering bars either by day (so that each group of bars has the frequencies of all of the behaviors) or by behavior (so that each group of bars has the data from all of the days); it would probably be best to show students examples of each.
USING AND ADAPTING THE ACTIVITY	
About the Activity	To do this activity, students need to understand what an ethogram is. Basically, an ethogram is the animal-behavior equivalent of a classroom-behavior checklist. In this activity, students will be asked to choose an animal that is being live-streamed and observe its behavior for 5–10 minutes. As they observe, students should note any repetitive patterns, and then define or describe those in writing and enter a descriptor for them in the table on the back of their activity page. The camera feeds provide some physical environmental information (for example, temperature) when it first starts (see the Explore screenshot above) and allows students to digitally capture an image for their report, if they want to. Students should observe the animal for 10–15 minutes on each of several days, and count the number of times each behavior occurs during those periods.
Scaling Down	To simplify this activity, you can focus on fewer activities. Students could just do a "behavioral repertoire" list, in which they just list the different actions that the animal performs, without counting them.
Scaling Up	For added complexity, students could construct a behavior-sequence chart, in which they list observed behaviors in the order they occur for a set period of time (usually short, such as 15–30 seconds). An example of a behavior-sequence might be, "Look left–look left–head shake–head shake–beak open–yawn–look left–head shake–still–still–loud call–quiet call–head shake."

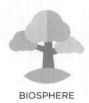

USING AND ADAPTING THE ACTIVITY (*continued*)	
Extending	**Influence of Area Ecology:** Investigate the ecology of the area in which the animal is found and aspects such as the animal's life history, types of food it eats, and reproductive behavior. This information can be used to understand and explain the behavior observations made by students when viewing the video. This information and observations made by the students can also be used in a literacy extension activity, such as writing a "Day in the life of your animal" narrative.
ASSESSMENT NOTES	
This is a good opportunity to introduce students to qualitative data, because information collected in this activity cannot be predicted and involves observation notes. Assessment should be based on the types of observations made and the detail provided, rather than the frequency. Students should be encouraged to provide thick, rich notes.	

Name: _____   BIOSPHERE

STUDENT HANDOUT: ANIMAL BEHAVIOR ETHOGRAMS

Activity Goal	In this activity, you will construct a behavior map of animal behavior, called an ethogram.
Technology Notes	You will access data on the Explore website at *http://explore.org*. There, click on the "Live Cams" link. Find an animal you want to observe, click on that image, and then bookmark it so you can find it again later. Your teacher might ask you to use an app instead.
Orientation Questions	Why do animals exhibit the behaviors they do? Why do they do some things over and over again? Think of an example of this.
Directions	1. Observe your live video feed for 10–15 minutes. Make a list of the behaviors you see your animal species or animal do during this time, and write a description of each behavior. (Screen-captured images can help with this.) Enter these in the behavior-sequence chart on the back of this page. 2. Observe how many times each of these behaviors happens during a 15-minute period on different days. Record the weather information. Take written notes describing what you observe in the 15-minute period (these are called *qualitative* observations). 3. After collecting this information on five or six days, look at the data and see whether there are patterns in the behaviors. 4. Complete the Analysis Questions and Reflection Activity sections.

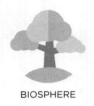

BIOSPHERE

BEHAVIOR-SEQUENCE CHART

Animal(s): _____ _____ Video description and location: _____	Temperature	Wind speed and direction	Precipitation (yes/no) and type	Amount of light	Cloud cover (%)	Behavior							Notes
Date and time													

Other notes:

ANALYSIS QUESTIONS

1. Which activity was most common? Were there any differences over the five (or more) days you recorded your information?

2. Why do you think those different behaviors were occurring? How might they help the animal (or its offspring or mate) to survive?

3. Which do you think was the most important behavior you observed? Why do you think that? If you had problems deciding on the most important behavior, discuss why.

4. What behavior did you expect to see but did not? Why?

5. Imagine that it started raining. How do you think rain would affect the behaviors you observed? Why?

6. How might the weather at other times of the year affect the animal you observed? Pick weather that is typical in another season and speculate about how that seasonal weather might influence the behavior(s) you observed.

REFLECTION ACTIVITY

Write a paragraph or two describing your observations and why you think those behaviors occurred over the period of your observations. Describe what you think about what you observed. Was there more or less activity than you expected? In thinking about your observations, discuss how an animal's life is different from yours.

CHAPTER 6

TEACHER NOTES: EMERGING OR DEVELOPED?

Learning Goal	Students will compare population dynamics in emerging and developed nations, including how those populations use natural resources.	
Disciplinary Core Ideas	<ul><li>Earth and human activity</li><li>Natural resources</li></ul>	
Science and Engineering Practices	<ul><li>Analyzing and interpreting data</li><li>Developing and using models</li></ul>	
Crosscutting Concepts	<ul><li>Systems and system models</li><li>Stability and change</li></ul>	
Background Information	Earth's human population is now well over 7 billion, yet not all of those people have the same living conditions. A demographic transition model compares birth rates and death rates as countries transition from being an emerging economy to being an industrialized, or developed, economy. In this activity, for the purpose of comparing populations in emerging versus developed economies, a country with a gross domestic product (GDP) per person ("per capita") of less than $10,000 U.S. dollars (USD) will be considered an emerging nation. One with a GDP per person of greater than $20,000 USD will be considered a developed country.	
DATA AND TECHNOLOGY		
Online Sources	<ul><li>Central Intelligence Agency (CIA) *World Factbook* website: *https://cia.gov/library/publications/resources/the-world-factbook.html*</li><li>QR Codes: See Table 6.1 (p. 138).</li></ul>	CIA *World Factbook* website screenshot on an iOS device
App and Device Sources	*World Factbook* app Platform: Android *World Facts* app Platform: iOS	*Source: https://cia.gov/library/publications/resources/the-world-factbook.*

BIOSPHERE

DATA AND TECHNOLOGY (continued)	
Technology Notes	The CIA *World Factbook* website has a responsive design and will work on small devices; however, its interactive map is Adobe Flash–based and will not work on some smartphone browsers. For example, on iPhones and iPads, it will work on the Puffin browser, but not on Safari. The data can still be accessed through the dropdown screen. The *World Factbook* and *World Facts* (iOS) apps are very large, because of the amount of data they contain. So although apps are available, students might not have enough storage on their devices for them and so using the website might be preferable.
About the Data	**Data Sampling:** No sampling issues are anticipated. **Data Type:** Most comparisons are a nominal (that is, unordered category) data type, except for the population pyramid, which is ordinal (ordered category) but which is plotted with horizontal bars nonetheless. **Data Issues:** No issues are anticipated. Most data are percentages (for which means should not be calculated, and there is no need for that).

USING AND ADAPTING THE ACTIVITY	
About the Activity	In this activity, students will compare an emerging nation to a developed nation using information obtained from CIA *World Factbook* website. Students will need to know how to calculate a percentage of a population to construct the population pyramid for each country. Students should have some familiarity with population pyramids and have access to calculators for the calculations.
Scaling Down	To simplify this activity and help with the math required to construct the population pyramid, set up a spreadsheet that will calculate the percentages automatically. Students can also work in pairs, with each partner gathering the data for one of the two countries being compared.
Scaling Up	For added complexity, students can compare data for several countries with different GDP levels (for example, < $5,000, $5,000–10,000 USD.). To help provide a more complete understanding of the economic differences, have students include additional data, for example, agriculture, urbanization, disease, and energy.
Extending	**A Day in the Life:** Have students use the data from the CIA *World Factbook* website and other information they gather through research to create a journal for a typical child of their own age in each country. Alternatively, students can present the journal in the form of videos or social media pages, such as simulated Facebook pages.

USING AND ADAPTING THE ACTIVITY *(continued)*	
Extending *(continued)*	**United Nations Simulation:** Divide the class into groups that represent either the emerging nation or the developed nation, and hold a mock United Nations assembly to address environmental issues identified in the activity. **Demographic Transition Model:** Have students determine where each nation fits on the Demographic Transition model, and explain how they can tell. **Enrichment Using Data:** Ask students to pick a variable for their chosen emerging country (for example, birth rate) and find historical data to track how this has changed over time. They could do the same with their chosen developed country.

ASSESSMENT NOTES

Generally, more-developed nations will have lower birth and death rates than less-developed ones. More-developed nations will also have better access to clean water and sanitation. Population pyramids for less-developed nations will have an expansive shape, whereas for more-developed nations, they might have more of a column-like shape.

Name: _____   BIOSPHERE

STUDENT HANDOUT: EMERGING OR DEVELOPED?

Activity Goal	In this activity, you will compare population dynamics in emerging and developed nations, including what natural resources are available and how the populations use them.
Technology Notes	You will use the Central Intelligence Agency (CIA) *World Factbook* website (*https://cia.gov/library/publications/resources/the-world-factbook*) or an app to find data for two countries.
Orientation Questions	• How would my life be different if I lived in an emerging nation? • What are the differences between emerging and developed countries?
Directions	1. On the CIA *World Factbook* website or using the *World Factbook* (Android) or *World Facts* (iOS) app, identify one emerging nation and one developed country, using a gross domestic product (GDP) per person ("per capita") of < $10,000 U.S. dollars (USD) to identify an emerging nation and of > $20,000 USD per person to identify a developed country. Try to pick countries no one else in your class has chosen. (Your teacher might decide to use a sign-up process to avoid repetition.) 2. Under the "People and Society" section, find the total population for each country. Then, use the "Age Structure" data to calculate the percentage of males and females in the population for each age range. Use this information to construct a population pyramid (using horizontal bars going left [% Male] and right [% Female] from the bold center line). 3. Under the "People and Society" and "Geography" sections, gather the remaining data for each country. Construct bar graphs to compare data for median age, improved drinking water, sanitation access, birth rate, death rate, and infant mortality rate. In list format, describe the natural resources, exports, and current environmental issues. 4. Display your Country Comparison Data with others in the class and take a "gallery walk" to complete the Analysis Questions section. 5. Complete the Conclusions and Reflection Question sections.

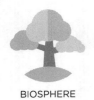

COUNTRY COMPARISON DATA

Emerging Country: _____   Developed Country: _____

Population Pyramids

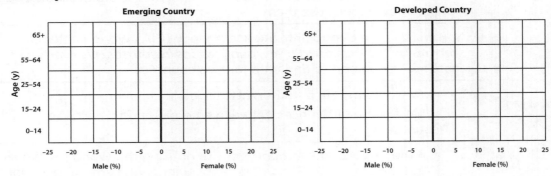

Population Dynamics Bar Graphs

Label the units on the *y*-axis for each graph. E = emerging; D = developed

Median Age	Improved Drinking Water	Sanitation Facility Access
E D	E D	E D
Birth Rate	**Infant Mortality Rate**	**Death Rate**
E D	E D	E D
Natural Resources Emerging: Developed:	**Exports** Emerging: Developed:	**Current Environmental Issues** Emerging: Developed:

ANALYSIS QUESTIONS

1. Summarize the differences between the two countries you compared.

2. What are three ways that emerging countries are similar?

3. What are three ways that developed countries are similar?

4. Of all the countries presented by students, which is the least developed? The most developed?

CONCLUSIONS

What are the key differences between emerging and developed countries?

REFLECTION QUESTION

How do the charts and graphs you created provide a model for understanding the differences between emerging and developed nations?

TEACHER NOTES: THIS LAND IS OUR LAND

Learning Goal	Students will explore long-term trends in land use using data from the U.S. Department of Agriculture (USDA).
Disciplinary Core Ideas	• Natural resources • Human impacts on Earth systems
Science and Engineering Practices	• Using mathematics and computational thinking • Obtaining, evaluating, and communicating information
Crosscutting Concepts	• Scale, proportion, and quantity • Stability and change
Background Information	Our planet has changed significantly over the past half-century. Since World War II, the population of the planet has doubled and the ways we use our land resources have changed. Population shifts have occurred because of changes in lifestyle, technology, and urban development. The USDA has collected land-use data since 1945, including cropland, grassland, forests, urban, and other uses. By analyzing these data, students can see not only how humans have affected Earth's systems, but also how land use changes over time.

DATA AND TECHNOLOGY

Online Sources	• 2007 USDA Major Land Uses Report: *www.ers.usda.gov/dataproducts/major-land-uses* • USDA *Soil and Water Resources Conservation Act (RCA) Interactive Viewer*: *www.nrcs.usda.gov/wps/portal/nrcs/rca/national/technical/nra/rca/ida* • U.S. Census Bureau *Historical Data*: *www.census.gov/popest/data/historical/index.html* • QR Codes: See Table 6.1 (p. 138).	USDA *Soil and Water RCA* website screenshot *Source:* USDA. *www.nrcs.usda.gov/wps/portal/nrcs/rca/national/technical/nra/rca/ida.*
App and Device Sources	No appropriate apps were located to supply the detailed information in the USDA database.	

	DATA AND TECHNOLOGY *(continued)*
Technology Notes	The 2007 USDA Major Land Uses (MLU) Report data are downloaded from that website as Excel spreadsheet files. Students can access the reports through their devices and then "mine" the reports for the desired data. The U.S. Census Bureau and USDA *Soil and Water RCA* websites have responsive design and will adjust to the size of the user's device. On the USDA *Soil and Water RCA* website, check "State" under "Scale," then "Natural Resources" under "Subjects"; then, click the desired state for a list of available reports.
About the Data	**Data Sampling:** No sampling issues are anticipated. **Data Type:** The comparison data are the nominal type (because there are only two "year" categories, so no other patterns would be discernible). A bar graph comparison for the different categories could also be done. **Data Issues:** Students must make sure the units for the categories across the two years being compared (for example, 1945, 2007) are the same. Different sources of information might use different units.
	USING AND ADAPTING THE ACTIVITY
About the Activity	Before beginning this investigation, students should have a firm understanding of how humans use land resources. They should also know how to calculate percentages and a percent increase or decrease. It is important that the teacher model how to retrieve data by projecting each website to guide students through acquiring the required data from for the activity.
Scaling Down	To simplify this activity, instead of having students plan and present data for different states, have individuals or groups collect and share data to contribute to the class for investigating only their home state. The state report could be the final outcome of the investigation or could be used as a modeling activity and to provide a scaffold to prepare students for individual or small-group investigations for the activity as written.
Scaling Up	For added complexity, have students calculate the percent change in land use—how much each category of land use (for example, cropland, forest, urban area) has increased or decreased over time. Students can also collect and report on interim data from the USDA and explore data changes by decade, rather than the overall period.

	USING AND ADAPTING THE ACTIVITY (*continued*)
Extending	**A Picture Is Worth a Thousand Words:** Students can add to their reports by doing extra research to find historical and current pictures of how farming, ranching, forestry, and urbanization have changed in their assigned state and adding these to their final product. **Climate Change:** Ask students to explore whether and how the climate has changed in each state (or in major cities in each state) using historical climate data from other resources, such as the Weather Underground website (*www.wunderground.com/history*) or the *Weather History Explorer* app. **Enrichment Using Data:** Students may collect data for multiple years (for example, 1945, 1955, 1965) to find out the patterns of change in the different categories.
	ASSESSMENT NOTES
	Data collected will vary widely, depending on the state selected for the investigation. Most states have seen an increase in urban development since 1945, at the expense of other land uses. Assessment for analysis questions should be based on the explanations offered in comparing different states, rather than just on the data provided.

Name: _____

BIOSPHERE

STUDENT HANDOUT: THIS LAND IS OUR LAND

Activity Goal	In this activity, you will explore changes in land use in a specific state during the latter half of the twentieth century. Then, you will participate in a "gallery walk" to compare your state's data to that of other states.
Technology Notes	You will access data from multiple websites to compile a presentation on land use in one state: • 2007 USDA Major Land Uses (MLU) Report: *www.ers.usda.gov/data-products/major-land-uses* • U.S. Census Bureau *Historical Data*: *www.census.gov/popest/data/historical/index.html* • U.S. Department of Agriculture (USDA) *Soil and Water Resources Conservation Act (RCA) Interactive Viewer*: *www.nrcs.usda.gov/wps/portal/nrcs/rca/national/technical/nra/rca/ida*
Orientation Questions	• Are land resources used the same way by people across the country? • How have the ways people use land resources changed over time?

Directions	1. Individually or in a group, as determined by your teacher, sign up for a specific state to research. Your teacher will tell you whether this may be any state or should be one in a specific geographic region(s).
	
	2. Access each website to retrieve the data according to the directions provided by your teacher.
	
	    a. USDA 2007 MLU Report: Collect data for 1945 and 2007 for each of their land-use categories: Cropland, grassland, forest-use, special use, urban area, and miscellaneous. Record these data in the table provided. Calculate the total land area for each time period. The total land area will be similar, but not identical, because of how the categories are defined and presented.
	
	    b. U.S. Census Bureau: Find the 2007 population of your research state from the "2000's" link. Use the "Pre-1980" link to find 1945 population data.
	
	    c. USDA *Soil and Water RCA Interactive Viewer*: Check "State" under "Scale" and both "Profiles" and "Natural Resources" under "Subjects." Then, click the desired state for a list of available reports and from that list, select "State Profile." Look over these data for interesting facts and information but do not add them to your data table, because they were prepared with different criteria than the other two data sets.
	
	3. Calculate the percentage of land use for each category for 1945 and for 2007, and enter these data in the Land-Use Data Table.

Directions (continued)	4. Complete the Data Analysis section by constructing a pie chart for each data set and a bar graph comparing the population totals of the two years.
	5. Prepare a poster that includes the state name and the land-use and population data you collected in graphical form.
	6. Go on a "gallery walk" to compare land use across the country. Answer the Analysis Questions.
	7. Complete the Conclusions and Reflection Question sections.

LAND-USE DATA TABLE

Using data from the USDA 2007 MLU Report website, calculate the percentage by dividing the acreage for each category by the total for each line.

State:				
Category	1945 (Acres)	1945 (%)	2007 (Acres)	2007 (%)
Cropland				
Grassland				
Forest-use				
Special use				
Urban area				
Miscellaneous				
Total		100		100
Population (in millions):	1945: _____		2007: _____	

DATA ANALYSIS PIE CHART AND BAR GRAPH

1945 Land Use	2007 Land Use	Population
◯	◯	1945 2007

ANALYSIS QUESTIONS

1. What changes have occurred in the state you researched? Describe them.

2. What other state is most like yours? What state is most different? Compare and contrast the trends you observe in _____ different states (you might want to use bar graphs).

3. How has technology contributed to the trends you observed in land use?

CONCLUSIONS

Describe the changes you observed in use of land resources by Americans during the latter half of the twentieth century. Do you notice any patterns in different regions (for example, Northeast, Southwest, and Midwest)? Cite evidence from the data to support your conclusions.

REFLECTION QUESTION

How did the use of graphs help you visualize trends in land resource use?

TEACHER NOTES: WILDFIRE!

Learning Goal	Students will determine whether there is a correlation between drought and wildfires using data from two states.
Disciplinary Core Ideas	• The roles of water in Earth's surface processes • Natural hazards
Science and Engineering Practices	• Analyzing and interpreting data • Constructing explanations and designing solutions
Crosscutting Concepts	• Cause and effect: Mechanism and explanation • Stability and change
Background Information	Usually about 100,000 wildfires are reported each year in the United States. Although drought and wildfires are separate hazards, they are related. Weather conditions such as drought can contribute to wildfires, which can begin in dry, hot conditions. As climates change, areas that become hotter can have increased rates of evaporation, leading to drier conditions.

DATA AND TECHNOLOGY

Online Sources	• *National Drought Monitor,* National Drought Mitigation Center website: *http://droughtmonitor.unl.edu/MapsAndData/DataTables.aspx* • National Interagency Fire Center website: *www.nifc.gov/fireInfo/fireInfo_statistics.html* • QR Codes: See Table 6.1 (p. 138).	*National Drought Monitor* website screenshot *Source: http://droughtmonitor.unl.edu.*
App and Device Sources	No appropriate apps were located for this activity for either data set.	
Technology Notes	• Students must access the data using the websites. Neither website has a responsive design; however, on both websites, the data are easily accessed and can be gathered using personal devices. • *National Drought Monitor,* National Drought Mitigation Center website: The link provided opens the site's Tabular Data Archive. From the left-side drop down menu, select "State" (defaults to "National"). The data are sortable by drought severity. • National Interagency Fire Center website: In the "Statistics" column, under "Historical year-end fire statistics by state," select the data year by year.	

DATA AND TECHNOLOGY *(continued)*

About the Data	**Data Sampling:** This activity requires students to sample drought data from a complex data set. The highest percentage of area experiencing extreme drought is to be considered the sample data point for each year. Instead of selecting the acreage of wildfires, students could instead work with the number of wildfires. **Data Type:** The drought and wildfire data both are interval–ratio (measured) types of data. **Data Issues:** The National Interagency Fire Center website data are annual, whereas the *National Drought Monitor* data are weekly, creating a mismatch between values. Calculating mean (average) and median values for each year would require an extra step but using those values might be more appropriate, because drought conditions vary across months within the same year. Note that the *x-y* graph will have two states on it, and a line of best fit will be required for each state, so students should use a different symbol (for example, * and +) for each data set.

USING AND ADAPTING THE ACTIVITY

About the Activity	Students should have a basic understanding of drought conditions and understand the difference between a prescribed burn and a wildfire. The drought data will be more difficult for students to work with because they are broken down by week, whereas the wildfire data are supplied by state. Students will make generalizations from drought data by sorting through the weekly data to find the highest percentage of extreme drought severity for each year.
Scaling Down	To simplify this activity, reduce the amount of data collected by having students work only with data from the single highest and lowest drought years, rather than across the entire data span and data compared using simpler graphs, such as a bar graphs. Model the activity by collecting the data from your home state as a class, and then have students research additional states in teams, with one student collecting the wildfire data and the other drought data.
Scaling Up	For added complexity, students can collect drought data by category (abnormally dry, moderate drought, severe drought, extreme drought, exceptional drought) and can compare different types of statistics, such as population affected rather than area in drought. In addition, data can be presented annually as a double line graph of data over time.

	USING AND ADAPTING THE ACTIVITY *(continued)*
Extending	**Does El Niño Play a Part?:** Have students research to see whether El Niño Southern Oscillation patterns (El Niño, La Niña) affect drought conditions in their area. **Climate Connections:** Students can research annual temperature and precipitation data in their states to determine the relationship between weather and wildfires. **Wildfire Safety:** Have students download the *American Red Cross Wildfire* app, research current wildfires, and then create a wildfire safety brochure. **Enrichment Using Data:** To classify the drought before comparing it to wildfire data, students can develop a drought-severity index for each year that takes into account the number of weeks of drought, the severity of the drought, and the highest level reached over the course of the year.
	ASSESSMENT NOTES

In general, expect to see a positive correlation between drought and wildfires; however, this might not always be the case because often other factors are involved as well.

Name: _____   BIOSPHERE

STUDENT HANDOUT: WILDFIRE!

Activity Goal	In this activity, you will explore the relationship between drought and wildfires.
Technology Notes	You will access data from two websites: 1. *National Drought Monitor*, National Drought Mitigation Center: *http://droughtmonitor.unl.edu/MapsAndData/DataTables.aspx* 2. National Interagency Fire Center: *www.nifc.gov/fireInfo/fireInfo_statistics.html*
Orientation Questions	• How do droughts affect ecosystems? • What conditions lead to an increase in the number of wildfires?
Directions	1. For this activity you will be research information from two states, as assigned by your teacher. One state may be your own. You will collect data for the most recent 12 years or for another range defined by your teacher. 2. *National Drought Monitor* website: Find the percent area in the "extreme drought" category for your state(s). From the left-side drop-down menu, select "State" (rather than "National") and then, from the middle drop-down menu, choose the state you are researching. Because the data are shown by week, you will search by year and then sort on the "Extreme Drought" column (red) to find the maximum percent area of extreme drought for that year. Enter those data into the data table. 3. National Interagency Fire Center website: In the "Statistics" column, under "Historical year-end fire statistics by state," find the data for the number of acres of wildland fires for your state for each year. Enter the data in the data table. 4. Complete the Data Analysis, Analysis Questions, Conclusions, and Reflection Question sections.

DATA TABLE

State:			State:		
Year	Maximum Area of Extreme Drought (%)	Wildland Fire Area (Acre)	Year	Maximum Area of Extreme Drought (%)	Wildland Fire Area (Acre)

DATA ANALYSIS

Construct a scatter plot to determine whether there is a correlation between drought conditions and the number of wildland fires for your two states. Use a different symbol for each state's data.

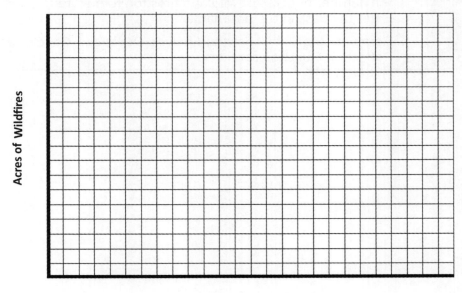

Maximum % Area Extreme Drought

ANALYSIS QUESTIONS

1. In what year was the drought the greatest in each state? How many acres were lost to wildfires in each of those years?

2. In what year was the drought the least in each state? How many acres were lost to wildfires in each of those years?

3. Why was drought used as an indicator of climate conditions in this activity?

4. Besides drought, what other variables could affect the number of wildfires?

5. Would you expect the impact of drought to be the same for different biomes (for example, desert, woodland)? Why or why not?

CONCLUSIONS

Construct an explanation that describes why wildfires might be more likely to occur during or after drought years. Use evidence you collected, if applicable, to support your conclusion.

REFLECTION QUESTION

With climates changing, some places are becoming hotter and drier. How might state officials change their preparedness for wildfires for states that are experiencing more droughts?

Table 6.1. Data sources for real-time biosphere investigations

Activity	Website	URL	QR Code
Behavior Ethograms	Explore	*http://explore.org*	
Emerging or Developed?	CIA *World Factbook*	*https://cia.gov/library/publications/resources/ the-world-factbook*	
This Land Is Our Land	2007 USDA Major Land Uses Report	*www.ers.usda.gov/data-products/major-land-uses*	
	U.S. Census Bureau *Historical Data*	*www.census.gov/popest/data/historical/index. html*	
	USDA *Resources Soil and Water Conservation Act (RCA) Interactive Viewer*	*www.nrcs.usda.gov/wps/portal/nrcs/rca/ national/technical/nra/rca/ida*	
Wildfire!	*National Drought Monitor,* National Drought Mitigation Center	*http://droughtmonitor.unl.edu/MapsAndData/ DataTables.aspx*	
	National Interagency Fire Center	*www.nifc.gov/fireInfo/fireInfo_statistics.html*	

Table 6.2. Additional biosphere-related data sources

Website	Address	QR Code
USDA *National Agriculture Statistics Service*	www.nass.usda.gov/Charts_and_Maps/Crops_County	
NOAA *Integrated Ocean Observing System Animal Telemetry Network*	http://oceanview.pfeg.noaa.gov/ATN	
Vegetation Condition Explorer	https://nassgeodata.gmu.edu/VegScape	

INVESTIGATIONS USING REAL-TIME GEOSPHERE DATA

The geosphere is composed of Earth's surface and interior. It includes our planet's core, mantle, and crust. It also includes rock and mineral resources and landforms and features, as well as the processes that shape Earth's surface. Much of what we know about Earth's interior is from seismic waves that travel through the planet at different speeds as they pass through materials of different density and composition. Satellites collect data from above, and other instruments collect and analyze data on and below Earth's surface.

When considering how to explore the geosphere using real-time data, earthquakes are most likely the first application that comes to mind. The U.S. Geological Survey (USGS) (*www.usgs.gov*) website is the primary source of data on earthquakes, volcanoes, and geomagnetism. Worldwide earthquake data usually include location, latitude, longitude, magnitude, and depth. The data are collected from all over the planet and reported in real time.

Although earthquake data can be used to locate plate-tectonic boundaries, it can also be used to explore other relationships. For example, does the depth of the earthquake provide information about the type of plate boundary? The ability to search archived data allows students to compare current and past earthquake activity to identify trends and construct possible explanations. For example, the USGS *Earthquake Hazards Program* (*http:// earthquake.usgs.gov/earthquakes/map*) website data for Oklahoma shows 51 earthquakes of magnitude 4.0 and greater during the five years from January 1, 2011, to November 30, 2015: 4 in 2011, 1 in 2012, 3 in 2013, 15 in 2014, and 28 in 2015 (see Figure 7.1, p. 142). They also show that nearly all of those earthquakes are very shallow, at depths of less than 10 km. From this, students could determine that the number of earthquakes has increased annually. The question for students to consider from these observations is what possible explanations would possibly account for this increase in earthquake activity.

The activities in this chapter provide examples of how to use geosphere data in the classroom, and provide resources for finding those data and suggestions for using them. One of our favorite resources for real-time plate-tectonics data is Rice University (*http:// tectonics.rice.edu/hs3.html*). Using their interactive calculator, students can find the velocity and direction of plate motion under their feet or anywhere else in the world. Data from

Figure 7.1. USGS five-year earthquake data for Oklahoma

Source: http://earthquake.usgs.gov/earthquakes/map.

this website shows that Seattle, Washington, on the North American plate, is moving at velocity of 23 mm/y in a direction of 250 degrees (azimuth angle of west-southwest). Just to the west by five degrees longitude in the Pacific Ocean, the Juan de Fuca plate is moving at nearly 21 mm/y in a direction of 49 degrees (azimuth angle of northeast). What do these data indicate about the type of plate motion occurring between these adjacent locations? By collecting data for various cities around the world, students can draw vectors on maps and create a visual model that illustrates the differences in plate motion.

The USGS *Volcano Hazards Program* (*http://volcanoes.usgs.gov*) monitors volcanoes in the United States; but although they have webcam coverage of various volcanoes, those more typically are shown on the website as still images from very recent feeds. The website also has subsites dedicated to the monitoring of individual volcanoes and that contain interesting information for educating the public and science communities. Overall, though, the *Volcano Hazards Program* website provides very little real-time or other data on U.S. volcanoes for either viewing or download. The *Global Volcanism Program* website of the Smithsonian Institution's National Museum of Natural History (*http://volcano.si.edu/index.cfm*) is a more-robust source of real-time volcano data, providing weekly updates on volcano events around the world. By correlating these data with the NASA *Global Sulfur Dioxide Monitoring* website (*http://so2.gsfc.nasa.gov*), students can explore the relationship between active volcanoes and atmospheric sulfur dioxide (SO_2).

The USGS does provide real-time data related to mineral resources and mines. Using the spatial-data service on the *Mineral Resources Data System* (*MRDS*) website (*http://mrdata. usgs.gov/mrds*), students can download information about mining and minerals for any location of the United States. For example, data from the site for Forsyth County, Georgia, shows there are 20 known mining locations there. Of these, 12 are gold-mining sites—most of them past producers and a few listed as prospects. Four are potential operations for mica, none actively producing. Two are actively producing facilities for sand, gravel, and crushed stone; one is a magnetite-mining prospect; and one is an iron-mining prospect.

Students can use these mining data with data from the USGS *National Geologic Maps Database* website (*http://ngmdb.usgs.gov/maps/mapview*) to construct an explanation about why those mineral resources are found in this region of the state, which is dominated by metamorphic and igneous rock. Additional mining data can be found on the Centers for Disease Control and Prevention (CDC) National Institute for Occupational Safety and Health (NIOSH) website (*www.cdc.gov/niosh/mining/statistics/allmining.html*), which provides some limited data on the location of mining locations and hazards associated with mining operations.

Tables 7.1 and 7.2 (pp. 169 and 170, respectively) list all digital resources used in this chapter.

REFERENCE

U.S. Geological Survey (USGS). *Earthquake Hazards Program*. *http://earthquake.usgs.gov/earthquakes/map*.

TEACHER NOTES: CONVERGENT OR DIVERGENT?

Learning Goal	Students will explore the relationship between earthquake depth and tectonic plate boundaries.
Disciplinary Core Ideas	• Earth materials and systems • Plate tectonics and large-scale system interactions
Science and Engineering Practices	• Analyzing and interpreting data • Constructing explanations and designing solutions
Crosscutting Concepts	• Systems and system models • Structure and function
Background Information	The focus of an earthquake is the location where the earthquake originates. It is seldom on Earth's surface; usually, it is on a fault within the crust. The epicenter is the place on the surface directly above the focus. Earthquakes occur at different depths and are classified by focus-depth range as shallow (0–70 km), intermediate (70–300 km), or deep (> 300 km). The depth of an earthquake provides information about the type of plate boundary it is near. Deep earthquakes are more often associated with subduction zones and convergent boundaries, whereas shallow earthquakes are associated with divergent and transform boundaries.

DATA AND TECHNOLOGY

Online Sources	• U.S. Geological Survey (USGS) *Earthquake Hazards Program* website: *http://earthquake.usgs.gov/earthquakes/map* • QR Code: See Table 7.1 (p. 169).	USGS *Earthquake Hazards Program* website smartphone screenshot
App and Device Sources	*Quakefeed* app Platform: iOS *EQInfo Global Earthquakes* app Platform: Android	*Source:* U.S. Geological Survey *Earthquake Hazards Program. http://earthquake.usgs. gov/earthquakes/map.*

DATA AND TECHNOLOGY (*continued*)	
Technology Notes	The USGS *Earthquake Hazards Program* website has a responsive design and is ideal for use on any device. The settings can be changed to view data for different magnitudes and periods of time. To collect enough data for the activity, students will need to change the settings to view data for earthquakes happening over a longer period of time.
About the Data	**Data Sampling:** A teacher might want to encourage students to identify an "even" sampling of earthquakes (marked in blue, red, or green); that is, to spread out their samples geographically; rather than clustering them. It might be helpful to specify that they should record earthquakes within a given distance (for example, an area running 1,600 km along a plate boundary).
	Data Type: Focal-depth data are the interval–ratio type and can be arithmetically summarized. The three focal-depth categories are the nominal data type, and so a bar graph could be used to compare them.
	Data Issues: The Richter scale is a measurement of earthquake strength, or magnitude, which is a special type of data for which a mean cannot be calculated (see Chapter 4); however, one can calculate the mean of the focal-depth measurements to use for comparison.
USING AND ADAPTING THE ACTIVITY	
About the Activity	For this activity, students must understand the types of plate boundaries (divergent, convergent, transform) as they look for relationships between depth and boundary type. Teachers should reinforce knowledge of geologic features by stressing that ridges and rifts occur at divergent boundaries and trenches occur at convergent boundaries. Many of the events reported in the data use these terms.
Scaling Down	To simplify this activity, assign students work in groups to research a different type of plate boundary or even a specific boundary. Then, have students share their reports with the class. When assigning groups, consider that not as many events occur at divergent boundaries. You might want to assign fewer students to these areas.
Scaling Up	For added complexity, provide students with a map that shows the locations of plate boundaries but not their types. The USGS *Earthquake Hazards Program* website does not include plate-boundary information (although some apps do). Students can use the data they collect to construct explanations about the type of plate motion occurring at each boundary.

	USING AND ADAPTING THE ACTIVITY (*continued*)
Extending	**Find the Boundaries!** Provide students with a map with no plate boundaries indicated and have them collect earthquake magnitude and depth data for that geographic area for a long time period (30 days or more). With the collected data, the students should be able to identify the type and location of most plate boundaries. **What's the Impact?** Have students research the newsworthy earthquakes that occur over the longer period of time to find out how they affect local populations. **Earthquake Safety:** Using the *American Red Cross Earthquake* app (*www.redcross.org/get-help/prepare-for-emergencies/mobile-apps*), have students construct a safety brochure about what to do in case of an earthquake, that includes basic information about the types of earthquakes and tectonic plate boundaries. **Enrichment Using Data:** Students could draw a bar graph comparing earthquakes of the three focal-depth categories, putting the raw data on it by hand so they get a sense of the variation around the mean (average).

ASSESSMENT NOTES

Most earthquakes occur near tectonic-plate boundaries, and most should occur near active faults. In general, earthquakes are deeper near convergent boundaries, where subduction is occurring, than near divergent or transform plate boundaries. Expect outliers in the data.

STUDENT HANDOUT: CONVERGENT OR DIVERGENT?

Activity Goal	In this activity, you will investigate whether there is a relationship between earthquake depth and the type of plate-tectonic boundary.
Technology Notes	Use data from the U.S. Geological Survey (USGS) *Earthquake Hazards Program* website (*http://earthquake.usgs.gov/earthquakes/map*) or an app recommended by your teacher to find the depth of earthquakes at different locations.
Orientation Questions	• How do earthquakes differ in the depth of their focus? • Is there a relationship between the depth of an earthquake's focus and the type of plate-tectonic boundary?

Directions	1. Open the website (or app) on your device.
	
	2. Under "Settings" (⚙), change the settings to show data for earthquakes from the past 30 days with a magnitude of 4.5 or higher.
	
	3. Use the Plate Tectonics Boundaries Map to identify convergent plate boundaries. From the data you retrieve using the website or app, pick 10 earthquakes along different convergent boundaries.
	
	    a. Mark their locations on the map, in red.
	
	    b. Record their location and depth on the data table.
	
	4. Repeat the process for 10 earthquakes along divergent plate boundaries, marking them in blue.
	
	5. Repeat again for 10 earthquakes along a transform boundary. You might have to adjust the magnitude settings to be able to see more events. Mark these in green.
	
	6. Complete the Analysis Questions, Conclusions, and Reflection Question sections.

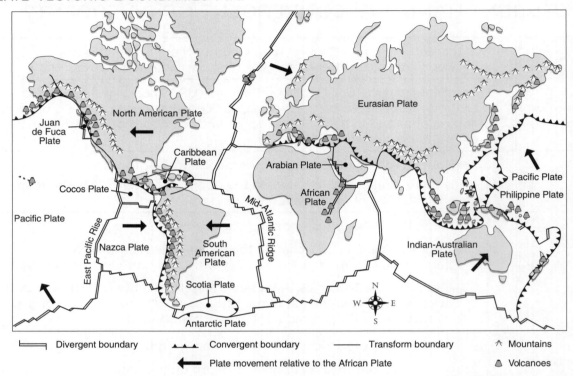

CHAPTER 7

GEOSPHERE

PLATE TECTONIC BOUNDARIES MAP

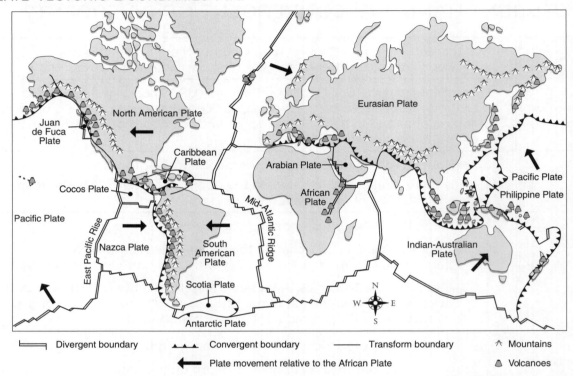

	Divergent boundary		Convergent boundary		Transform boundary		Mountains
			Plate movement relative to the African Plate				Volcanoes

Source: © Province of British Columbia. All rights reserved. Reproduced with permission of the Province of British Columbia.

DATA TABLE

Convergent Boundary		Divergent Boundary		Transform Boundary	
Location	Depth (_____)	Location	Depth (_____)	Location	Depth (_____)
Mean Depth		Mean Depth		Mean Depth	

NATIONAL SCIENCE TEACHERS ASSOCIATION

ANALYSIS QUESTIONS

The focus of an earthquake is the location where the earthquake originates. An earthquake is categorized by the depth of its focus as shallow (0–70 km deep), intermediate (70–300 km) or deep (> 300 km).

1. What can the depth of an earthquake's focus tell you about the type of tectonic plate boundary it is most likely associated with?

2. At which type of plate boundary do the deepest earthquakes occur? Are most earthquakes at this boundary considered shallow, intermediate, or deep?

3. At which type of plate boundary do the shallowest earthquakes occur? Are most earthquakes at this boundary considered shallow, intermediate, or deep?

4. How do your data compare to data of your classmates?

CONCLUSIONS

Using what you know about the different type of tectonic plate boundaries, construct an explanation that discusses at which type of plate boundary the deepest earthquakes are most likely to occur and why.

REFLECTION QUESTION

How does Earth's structure provide insight into where the deepest earthquakes are most likely to occur?

TEACHER NOTES: RADON MAPPER

Learning Goal	Students will learn about the radiation levels in their state and county and compare them to levels in two other states. Teaching about radon addresses a safety issue and relates to content knowledge about radiation and geology.
Disciplinary Core Ideas	• Biogeology • Natural hazards
Science and Engineering Practices	• Analyzing and interpreting data • Developing and using models
Crosscutting Concepts	• Scale, proportion, and quantity • Energy and matter: Flows, cycles, and conservation
Background Information	Radon is an invisible, radioactive gas that comes from soil and rocks. It is naturally occurring, odorless, and colorless. It can become a health hazard if it accumulates to higher concentrations in our homes, schools, and offices. Determining the level of radon in such locations is important, because radon is the leading cause of lung cancer in people who have never smoked (and the second-leading cause of lung cancer in the United States overall). Groundwater has a higher concentration of radon than surface water, because radon is produced by the radioactive decay of radium that is present in rocks. Radon in homes usually enters the building directly from the soil that is in contact with the lower parts of the buildings (for example, basements); cracks in a building's foundation can increase radon entry. Also, high levels of radon in the water supply can raise radon levels in the air in buildings. The U.S. Environmental Protection Agency (EPA) believes any radon level above 4 picocuries per liter of air (pCi/L) requires further monitoring and/or mitigating action.

DATA AND TECHNOLOGY

Online Sources	• EPA *Radon* website: *www.epa.gov/radon/find-information-about-local-radon-zones-and-radon-programs* • State-Radon website: *http://state-radon.info/statelist.html* • QR Codes: See Table 7.1 (p. 169).	EPA *Radon* website screenshot
App and Device Sources	No appropriate apps were located for this activity.	*Source:* U.S. Environmental Protection Agency. *www.epa.gov/radon/find-information-about-local-radon-zones-and-radon-programs.*

DATA AND TECHNOLOGY *(continued)*	
Technology Notes	The EPA *Radon* website has a responsive design—it works on small devices and its page "snaps" to the screen size of the device; however, it can be challenging to work with the map on a small screen. The State-Radon website does not have a responsive design, but works well on small devices.
About the Data	**Data Sampling:** Sampling is relatively straightforward because students are counting the number of counties at each radon risk level in three states. **Data Type:** Comparisons of radon-level frequencies between states are nominal level. **Data Issues:** None.

USING AND ADAPTING THE ACTIVITY	
About the Activity	Students will use the EPA *Radon* website to record and summarize radon data for three states in the data table of their activity handout. Teachers might want to have a preceding lesson on the types and sources of radioactivity, why radioactivity is a risk factor for humans, and how exposure to radioactivity can be mitigated. Students will need to be aware that the EPA categorizes radon exposure into three risk levels, according to the level of radon radioactivity involved.
Scaling Down	To simplify this activity, have students examine the radon levels in just their own state.
Scaling Up	For added complexity, students could be asked to complete a more complex table that compares rock types commonly found in areas with low, medium, and high radon levels.
Extending	**Income Versus Radon Risk:** Have the students pick 10 to 20 random counties for each of the risk zones and then use U.S. Census Bureau data (for example, *www.census.gov/did/www/saipe/data/interactive/saipe.html?s_appName=saipe&map_yearSelector=2014&map_geoSelector=mhi_c&s_measures=mhi_snc*) to examine the relationship between "Median Household Income (state/county)" and general radon risk. (This is graphed with income on the *y*-axis and three tic marks representing zones 1, 2, and 3 on the *x*-axis. A mark for income would be recorded for each county over the appropriate zone.) **Public Service Announcement Video:** Have students make a radon public service announcement video for their school announcements that includes basic information about radon, as well as information on radon risk in their area, how to check for radon levels in the home, what the risks of radon exposure are over time, and what to do if radon risk is a problem where they live.

USING AND ADAPTING THE ACTIVITY *(continued)*	
Extending *(continued)*	**Enrichment Using Data:** Students could be divided into groups that examine radon levels in different regions of the United States—North, South, East, West, and Central—and then report their findings to each other.
ASSESSMENT NOTES	
Radon levels will vary greatly, depending on the geology of the area. Students should be assessed on how they present and describe the differences in radon levels in the areas selected.	

Name: _____   GEOSPHERE

STUDENT HANDOUT: RADON MAPPER

Activity Goal	In this activity, you will examine data maps to determine radon levels in the counties of different states.
Technology Notes	Obtain data for this activity from data maps on two websites: 1. U.S. Environmental Protection Agency (EPA) *Radon*: *www.epa.gov/ radon/find-information-about-local-radon-zones-and-radon-programs* 2. State-Radon: *http://state-radon.info/statelist.html*
Orientation Questions	• How are radon maps produced? • What information is included on the data map on the EPA *Radon* website?
Directions	1. Using the EPA map, count the number of counties with each level of radon (in each risk zone) in your state. (Clicking the "i" icon in the middle of the state brings up a pop-up window, on the bottom of which is a larger scale state map showing the counties.) Pick two other states for comparison, and repeat. Record this information in the Table of State/County Radon-Gas Risk in this handout. 2. Using those counts, calculate the percentage of counties in each state at each radon zone and complete the bar graph comparing these data for each state. 3. Do some basic research on radon, why it carries a risk for humans, what risk it carries, and how those risks can be reduced. 4. Complete the Analysis Questions, Conclusions, and Reflection Question sections.

GEOSPHERE

CHAPTER 7

TABLE OF STATE/COUNTY RADON-GAS RISK

	Your State: _____		Comparison State 1: _____		Comparison State 2: _____	
Number of Counties in State:	_____		_____		_____	
Risk Category	Number of Counties	% of Total Counties	Number of Counties	% of Total Counties	Number of Counties	% of Total Counties
Zone 1 (> 4 pCi/L)						
Zone 2 (2 to 4 pCi/L)						
Zone 3 (< 2 pCi/L)						
Total:						
pCi/L = picocuries per liter of air						

BAR GRAPH

Percentage of Counties

100
90
80
70
60
50
40
30
20
10
0

Zone 3 Zone 2 *Zone 1   Zone 3 Zone 2 *Zone 1   Zone 3 Zone 2 *Zone 1

_____ Your State _____   _____ Comparison State 1 _____   _____ Comparison State 2 _____

*Zone 1 has the highest radon concentration, at > 4 pCi/L.

NATIONAL SCIENCE TEACHERS ASSOCIATION

ANALYSIS QUESTIONS

1. How does your state compare to the other two states for radon risk?

2. Find a geologic map. Do the three states have different types of rock? Does rock type relate to radon level? Why did you conclude this?

3. Is radon gas more or less dense than air? What does this mean for where you might find high radon levels in a house?

4. Do a little research! After whom is the radiation unit "curie" named? Why was that person chosen to have the radioactivity unit named after them?

5. The EPA states that "Homes with elevated levels of radon have been found in all three zones." If your house is in a zone 3 county, does that mean your house has a safe level of radon? Explain your answer.

6. What does the EPA recommend be done to each house to make sure it does not have high radon levels?

CONCLUSIONS

Compare your findings with those of others in the class and draw some general conclusions about radon, where it is found, and risks in different geographic areas.

REFLECTION QUESTION

How might the amount of radon risk influence where you decide to live in the future?

TEACHER NOTES: TECTONIC PLATE SHUFFLE

Learning Goal	Students will develop a model that illustrates that the tectonic plates are moving in different directions on Earth's surface
Disciplinary Core Ideas	• Earth materials and systems • Plate tectonics and large-scale system interactions
Science and Engineering Practices	• Developing and using models • Using mathematics and computational thinking
Crosscutting Concepts	• Systems and system models • Stability and change
Background Information	Earth's crust is divided into dozens of plates. Sources vary on this, but our planet's crust is divided into as many as 58 tectonic plates that move 2.5–15 cm/y. These plates slide in different directions across the Earth's asthenosphere, and as they move, they slowly reshape the surface of the planet.

DATA AND TECHNOLOGY		
Online Sources	• Rice University *Plate Motion Calculator*: *http://tectonics.rice.edu/hs3.html* • QR Code: See Table 7.1 (p. 169)	Rice University *Plate Motion Calculator* screenshot Calculated from HS3-NUVEL1A Reference: Gripp, A.E & Gordon R.G., Young tracks of hotspots and current plate velocities, Geophys. J. Int., 150, 321–361, 2002. RICE Name of Plate: [Pacific] Latitude [degrees N(+), S(-)] 21 Longitude [degrees E(+), W(-)] -157 → [Execute calculation] Plate Angular Velocity Components: Pole Latitude -61.467 Pole Longitude 90.326 Omega (degrees/Myr) 1.0613 Speed and Direction for input Location: Rate (mm/yr) 102.91 ◄——— Distance Azimuth (cw from N) -59.7 ◄——— Direction *Source: http://tectonics.rice.edu/hs3.html.*
App and Device Sources	*Coordinates* app for finding latitude and longitude Platform: iOS	
	N 45, E 25 *Map Coordinates* app for finding latitude and longitude Platform: Android	
	No apps with plate motion calculators were located.	
Technology Notes	Several websites are available that can be used for calculating tectonic plate motion. The Rice University *Plate Motion Calculator* is one of the simplest, having the fewest input fields as well as a responsive design that works well on a smartphone or tablet. It is important to note that the latitude input field requires the use of a plus sign for northern latitudes and a minus sign for southern latitudes, and the longitude input field requires the use of a plus sign for locations east of the prime meridian and a minus sign for those west of the prime meridian.	

DATA AND TECHNOLOGY *(continued)*	
About the Data	**Data Sampling:** The simplest use of the website tool is to choose a tectonic plate and execute the calculation without entering a longitude and latitude. Each velocity measure can be compared. **Data Type:** The data are the nominal data type (the tectonic plates are all independent from each other), and could be graphed; however, no graphing is being done in this activity. **Data Issues:** Data will be entered on a map with an arrow line that represents the direction of the plate movement. For students to use the line length to represent the amount of movement, scaling will be needed. (For example, some plates move > 100 mm/y, which would be difficult to represent with a 1:1 vector line unless students had a large map.) The activity suggests a 1:0.5 ratio. Otherwise, students must calculate a ratio (a divisor) that works for the size of their maps (and teachers might have to help them with this), so that the lines all fit on the map.
USING AND ADAPTING THE ACTIVITY	
About the Activity	Several challenges could arise, depending on students' mapping skills and understanding of vectors; students are probably less familiar with drawing vectors. A vector is an arrow that shows the magnitude and direction of a variable. Start at the point and draw in the direction of the azimuth (degrees clockwise from north). To fit the page, each vector must be drawn at 50% of scale, that is, at half as long as the rate or distance of plate motion it represents. Higher rates (distance) mean longer arrows. This activity could be used to introduce students to plate tectonics by having them identify different types of plate tectonic boundaries (convergent, divergent, transform), based on the map they create.
Scaling Down	To simplify this activity, preselect representative cities for students to collect data on, rather than allowing them to make their own list. Teachers might also want to provide the latitude and longitude information in advance. To make the vectors easier to illustrate, have students draw an arrow with the correct orientation (azimuth), without concern about the vector's proportion (length). The model produced will allow students to see the core concept, that Earth's tectonic plates are moving in different directions; however, it will be limited in that students will not be able to compare velocities.
Scaling Up	For added complexity, provide students with a map that does not show tectonic plate boundaries and have them determine where those boundaries are based on the data they collect.

USING AND ADAPTING THE ACTIVITY *(continued)*	
Extending	**Earth in 10,000 Years:** Ask students to assume that the tectonic plates will continue in the same direction and velocity for the next 100,000 years. (Be sure they also know that is unlikely and tectonic plate movements are dynamic and constantly changing.) Based on this activity's assumption, what might Earth's surface look like in 100,000 years? How might local climates change? **Enrichment Using Data:** Students might find it useful to draw a bar graph of the yearly tectonic plate movement, ordered from least to most, to get an understanding of the variation in this among the plates each year.
ASSESSMENT NOTES	
Depending on the locations chosen, different places on the same plate can be moving in different directions. One of the most important things to assess is whether the vectors are accurately drawn based on the data collected.	

Name: _____

STUDENT HANDOUT: TECTONIC PLATE SHUFFLE

Activity Goal	In this activity, you will develop a model that illustrates tectonic plate movement at different locations on Earth's surface.
Technology Notes	Gather data using the Rice University *Plate Motion Calculator* (*http://tectonics.rice.edu/hs3.html*) and use those data to construct vectors (that is, lines with an arrow) on a map to illustrate the velocity and direction of tectonic plate movement.
Orientation Questions	• Are all tectonic plates moving in the same direction or at the same rate? • Does every location on the same plate move at the same speed and in the same direction? • How can vectors be used to help visualize data?

Directions	1. Identify 12 cities that currently exist, one on each of the major tectonic plates with human populations that are shown on the map for this activity (that is, exclude plates that are under water, such as the Nazca Plate).
	
	2. Find the latitude and longitude for each city by using an internet search engine (for example, Google) or an app suggested by your teacher.
	
	3. Find the rate and azimuth for each city/plate by using the Rice University online Plate Motion Calculator through a web browser on a computer, smartphone, or tablet. In the calculator, select the plate on which the city is located, enter the city's latitude and longitude coordinates, and then click "Execute Calculation."
	
	4. Record all of these data in the table provided.
	
	5. Complete the Data Analysis by constructing vectors on the map, based on the data.
	
	    a. Mark the approximate location for each city on the map.
	
	    b. Cut out the picture of the compass in this handout and place it on each location, with the compass center on each city's location and the compass "N" pointing upward. Mark the direction the plate is moving based on the azimuth data.
	
	    c. Draw an arrow from the location of the city outward and in the direction the plate is moving. This arrow should be drawn at 50% of scale, that is, half as long as the rate or distance of plate motion, in millimeters (mm).
	
	6. Complete the Analysis Questions, Conclusion, and Reflection Question sections.

DATA TABLE

City	Tectonic Plate	Latitude	Longitude	Rate (Velocity) (mm/yr)	Azimuth (Direction)
Example: Honolulu, Hawaii, United States	Pacific	+21	−157	102.9	59.7

DATA ANALYSIS

Draw vectors on the map provided according to the directions.

COMPASS

You will use the compass to identify the azimuth of each location on the map. Azimuth is a measure of angular distance, with 360 degrees in a circle. It corresponds to the directions on a compass.

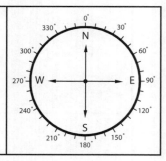

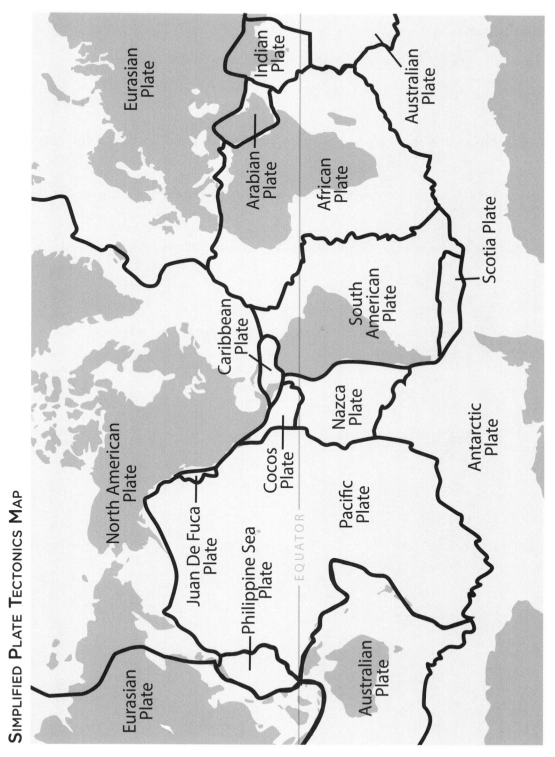

SIMPLIFIED PLATE TECTONICS MAP

Source: U.S. Geological Survey, pubs.usgs.gov/gip/dynamic/slabs.html

Analysis Questions

Compare your map to other students' maps to help answer these questions.

1. Are all plates moving in the same direction or at the same rate?

2. Are all locations on the same plate moving in the same direction or at the same velocity?

3. What evidence in your data suggests convergence or divergence at tectonic boundaries?

4. Which locations appear to be moving at the fastest rate? At the slowest rate?

Conclusions

How does the model you created help illustrate the action of plate tectonics?

Reflection Question

How would the theory of plate tectonics change if the data showed no movement or random directions for locations on the same plate?

TEACHER NOTES: VOLCANO RISK

Learning Goal	Students will explore volcanoes in the United States and relate them to tectonic plates in Earth's crust.	
Disciplinary Core Ideas	• Earth materials and systems • Plate tectonics and large-scale system interactions	
Science and Engineering Practices	• Planning and carrying out investigations • Constructing explanations and designing solutions	
Crosscutting Concepts	• Patterns • Energy and Matter: Flows, cycles, and conservation	
Background Information	According to the U.S. Geological Survey (USGS) website (*https://volcanoes.usgs.gov/vhp/nvews.html*), the United States has over 160 active volcanoes, more than 50 of which are designated "high priority threats"; almost 20 of those are considered "highest priority." Volcanoes are found where tectonic plates meet or at "hot spots" where Earth's crust is thin. The threat level of a volcano is determined by its potential to erupt, the local population, its past eruption frequency, and the size of its past eruptions.	
DATA AND TECHNOLOGY		
Online Sources	• USGS *Volcano Hazards Program* website: *http://volcanoes.usgs.gov/index.html* • QR Code: See Table 7.1 (p. 169).	*Volcanoes: Map, Alerts, Earthquakes and Ash Clouds* app screenshot
App and Device Sources	*Volcanoes: Map, Alerts, Earthquakes and Ash Clouds* app Platforms: Android, iOS	*Source:* Barouline, S. *Volcanoes: Map, Alerts, Earthquakes and Ash Clouds* app.

DATA AND TECHNOLOGY *(continued)*	
Technology Notes	The USGS *Volcano Hazards Program* website does not have a responsive design and is difficult to use on small devices; however, the *Volcanoes* app is excellent, especially for volcanoes that are well-known. The app does not provide extensive data for all locations. Look for the "i" symbol (shown on the screenshot from the app) to find volcanoes about which the app has additional information. There are several other free apps that can be used as an alternative. Students will likely need to use the web browser on their devices to access those additional research components.
About the Data	**Data Sampling:** Students should select their volcanoes so that they are spread out in different areas. **Data Type:** Comparisons of different volcano-eruption frequencies over time are interval–ratio (that is, by time); however, comparisons of volcanoes (using a bar chart to show eruption frequency) are nominal-level. **Data Issues:** Where data are available, most should be fairly straightforward. Where data are not available, students might have to do counts and estimates of populations within the stated range.
USING AND ADAPTING THE ACTIVITY	
About the Activity	Ideally, students will understand plate tectonics and earthquakes before examining the topic of volcanoes. In this activity, students will pick five active volcanoes and assess the risk from each one by looking at its history of volcanic activity, location in relation to local population numbers, and ash and/or gas risk (which requires an understanding of prevailing winds). There are five volcano observatories in the United States (*http://volcanoes.usgs.gov/vhp/observatories.html*). One difficulty that might arise for students is that the different observatories provide varying information, each reporting relevant data for volcanoes in that jurisdiction. For instance, the Alaska observatory provides a detailed visual depiction of known historical volcanic events for each volcano; others might provide that information but not in a format that is as easily accessed.
Scaling Down	To simplify this activity, rather than allowing students to choose the volcanoes, the teacher can assign groups of students to report on volcanoes found in each of the five U.S. volcano observatories (*http://volcanoes.usgs.gov/vhp/observatories.html*). Alternatively, each student could be assigned one volcano to report on to the rest of the class, and the class collectively could design a way of evaluating risk. Population size near the volcano could be a risk category (small, medium, large, very large), with population numbers per category specified by the teacher.

USING AND ADAPTING THE ACTIVITY *(continued)*	
Scaling Up	For added complexity, students could integrate plate movement into the estimation of volcanic risk. Earthquake activity in the area of each volcano could also be depicted on the graph to identify a possible correlation.
Extending	**Local Historical Stories:** The teacher might see whether there are any indigenous elders in the area of the studied events who have historical stories about earthquakes or volcanic eruptions in their region. (Of course, this might not be possible in areas of the United States that are less prone to these events). **Enrichment Using Data:** Students could be asked to relate volcanic activity to direction of plate movement and to crust thickness.

ASSESSMENT NOTES

Depending on the specific volcanoes chosen for this investigation, students might see a variety of data. Some volcanoes are less active than others; those with more frequent events and higher nearby populations should be assigned higher risk.

Name: _____

STUDENT HANDOUT: VOLCANO RISK

Activity Goal	In this activity, you will pick five active volcanoes, collect information about them, and evaluate each regarding its the threat level.
Technology Notes	Data will come from the *U.S. Volcanoes and Current Activity Alerts* page on the U.S. Geological Survey (USGS) *Volcano Hazards Program* website at *http://volcanoes.usgs.gov/index.html*. Your teacher might ask you to use an app instead.
Orientation Questions	• How was the map of volcanically active areas produced? • What type of information might be useful to know about volcanoes?
Directions	**Ground-based Volcano Alert Levels** Normal Advisory Watch Warning **Aviation Color Codes** Green Yellow Orange Red →Increasing level of concern→ △ Unassigned (insufficent monitoring to make assessment) *Source: http://volcanoes.usgs.gov/index. html.* — On the USGS *Volcano Hazards Program* website, alert levels for volcanoes are indicated by green, yellow, orange, and then red triangles that represent increasing level of concern.

Directions (continued)

1. Collect data about five active volcanoes from the USGS *Volcano Hazards Program* website or an app, including the recent and historical activity. Try to choose your volcanoes so that they are apart from one another and your data are spread out on the map. Record these data on the Data Table provided.

2. Using other sources, determine how many people live within 25 miles of the volcano area. Record these data on the Data Table provided.

3. Using other sources, determine the direction that the prevailing winds blow in the area. Record these data on the Data Table provided.

4. Using the provided blank line graph, draw a graph showing the number of volcanic events for each volcano. Define the year range for "recent" and "historical." Use the code for each volcano as given in the Data Table. Put the code at the height of the scale you draw on the left axis to depict the total number of volcanic events in each time period. Note: Do not put the code for any time period where there were no volcanic events.

5. Complete the Analysis Questions, Conclusions, and Reflection Question sections.

GEOSPHERE

Data Table

Volcano Name	Volcano Code	Volcano Location	Number of Recent Volcanic Events	Number of Recent Eruptions	Number of Historical Volcanic Events	Population Within 25-Mile Radius	Prevailing Wind Direction	Est. Downwind Population at Risk	Threat Risk
	V1								
	V2								
	V3								
	V4								
	V5								

Graph

Date ranges:	Recent: _____ to _____	Historical: _____ to _____

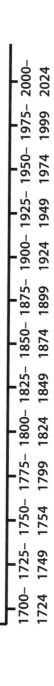

Number of volcanic events

1700–1724 1725–1749 1750–1754 1775–1799 1800–1824 1825–1849 1850–1874 1875–1899 1900–1924 1925–1949 1950–1974 1975–1999 2000–2024

Analysis Questions

1. Which of your volcanoes has been most active recently? Historically?

2. Which of your volcanoes has the greatest risk of eruption? Why do you believe that? What evidence did you use to come to that conclusion? Rank your volcanoes from highest risk to lowest risk on the basis of that evidence.

3. Does being volcanically inactive for a long time create a higher risk of eruption or a lower one? How might the level of recent volcanic activity relate to earthquake activity? To tectonic plate movement?

4. How does Earth's crust being thinner at some places relate to volcanic activity? What relationship might this have to some groups of volcanoes looking as though they are in a line?

5. What types of gasses can come out of a volcano? How does this relate to prevailing winds? What role might these gasses and volcanic ash play in climate change?

Conclusions

Compare the location of active volcanoes to the location of plate tectonic boundaries. Construct an explanation that describes the relationship between tectonic plate boundaries and the presence and activity of volcanoes.

Reflection Question

Does the pattern of recent volcanic activity help predict future events? Why or why not?

Table 7.1. Data sources for real-time geosphere investigations

Activity	Website	URL	QR Code
Convergent or Divergent?	USGS *Earthquake Hazards Program*	*http://earthquake.usgs.gov/earthquakes/map*	
Radon Mapper	EPA *Radon*	*www.epa.gov/radon/find-information-about-local-radon-zones-and-radon-programs*	
	State-Radon	*http://state-radon.info/statelist.html*	
Tectonic Plate Shuffle	Rice University *Plate Motion Calculator*	*http://tectonics.rice.edu/hs3.html*	
Volcano Risk	USGS *Volcano Hazards Program*	*http://volcanoes.usgs.gov*	

Table 7.2. Other sources for real-time geosphere data

Website	Address	QR Code
Centers for Disease Control and Prevention (CDC) The National Institute for Occupational Safety and Health (NIOSH), All Mining Statistics	www.cdc.gov/niosh/mining/statistics/allmining.html	
Global Volcanism Program, Smithsonian Institution National Museum of Natural History	http://volcano.si.edu/index.cfm	
USGS	www.usgs.gov	
USGS *National Geologic Map Database*	http://ngmdb.usgs.gov/ngmdb/ngmdb_home.html	
USGS *National Geologic Maps Database* (mapview)	http://ngmdb.usgs.gov/maps/mapview	
USGS *Mineral Resources Data System (MRDS)*	http://mrdata.usgs.gov/mrds	
NASA *Global Sulfur Dioxide Monitoring*	http://so2.gsfc.nasa.gov	

8

INVESTIGATIONS USING REAL-TIME HYDROSPHERE DATA

The hydrosphere is the watery part of Earth. Whether the water is on the surface as rivers, oceans, and streams; floating aloft as a cloud; or under the surface as an aquifer, it is part of the hydrosphere. Earth's surface is approximately 70% water, and data on all that water are collected by satellites and surface instruments. Satellites can track sea-surface temperature; glacier movements; changes in water-table levels, salinity, and tides; and many other data. Ground instruments can measure small changes in the dissolved oxygen level in a river, the velocity of water in a stream, and the depth of water in a dam. For the purposes of this book, we include the cryosphere (frozen water) in this chapter.

An important website for real-time ocean-surface data is the National Oceanic and Atmospheric Administration (NOAA) National Data Buoy Center (NDBC) (*www.ndbc.noaa.gov*). Using this website, students can explore real-time data for ocean waves, wind speed, water temperature, and more, from buoys and monitoring stations. As suggested in Chapter 1, students can use NDBC data to investigate how wind speed affects wave height, but they also can use it to explore other relationships. Video feeds can be used to collect observational data on Earth's hydrosphere. NOAA provides buoy cams in a few locations, but those provide visual data for exploring various ocean surface conditions. Marina and dock cameras can also be a rich source of visual, real-time data.

NOAA also provides tide data from tide stations all along the U.S. coastline (*http://tidesandcurrents.noaa.gov/tsunami*). Students could use these data to compare and contrast tidal patterns for different locations, or could collect data for different periods over several weeks and determine the impact of Moon phases on tides. NOAA also has the *nowCOAST* web page (*http://nowcoast.noaa.gov*), which goes beyond tide data and includes coastal observations, forecasts, and warnings, including forecasts of algae blooms.

Although NOAA does provide some real-time data for inland waterways, the ultimate resource for river and stream data is the U.S. Geological Survey (USGS) *National Water Information System* website (*http://waterdata.usgs.gov/nwis/rt*). Information for thousands of streams and rivers across the country is provided in real time with a color-coded system showing above normal streamflow in blues with below normal in reds (see Figure 8.1, p. 172). Links to each monitoring station provide a wealth of data, including discharge in cubic feet per second (cfs), drainage area, and water temperature. The USGS

Figure 8.1. Streamflow locations from USGS

Wednesday, November 02, 2016 17:30ET

Source: U.S. Geological Survey. *http://waterdata.usgs.gov/nwis/rt.*

WaterQualityWatch website (*http://waterwatch.usgs.gov/wqwatch*) provides information on fewer locations, but provides current quality data for water, including temperature, pH, turbidity, and levels of nitrates and dissolved oxygen. With these data, students can conduct investigations into the relationship between weather and streamflow, compare data from different monitoring stations on the same river, and explore environmental factors that can affect stream health.

Figure 8.2. USGS groundwater data for groundwater site 3426301194423014 in Santa Barbara, California

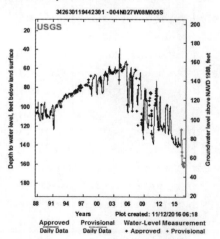

Source: U.S. Geological Survey. *http:// groundwaterwatch.usgs.gov/net/ ogwnetwork.asp?ncd=rtn*

The USGS also monitors groundwater (*http:// groundwaterwatch.usgs.gov/net/ogwnetwork. asp?ncd=rtn*), providing data that students can use to investigate the depth of multiple locations and explore variables that affect the water table (for example, weather and seasonal fluctuations) to better understand droughts. Figure 8.2 is a graph from the site that shows the water table height at a well in Santa Barbara, California, over the past 20 years. The effects of a recent drought in California on the water table are evident, and the site allows analysis of historical trends. In addition, the USGS *Groundwater Watch* website provides satellite views of well locations, giving students an opportunity to see the location of each site and investigate more complex relationships among topography, land use, and groundwater.

Figure 8.3. NSIDC data for Arctic Sea ice levels

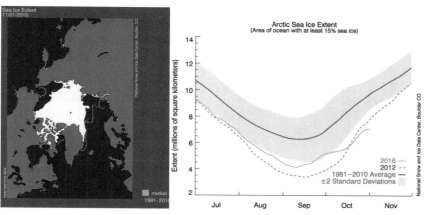

Source: National Snow and Ice Data Center. *https://nsidc.org/arcticseaicenews.*

The NASA National Snow and Ice Data Center (NSIDC) website (*http://nsidc.org*) provides nearly real-time data on the cryosphere. Students can view sea ice levels in the Arctic and Antarctic and observe temporal trends. Figure 8.3 shows current Arctic sea ice levels, which can be graphically compared to prior years. Of particular interest is its repository of more than 30 years' worth of satellite observations of Arctic change, which provides satellite images of sea ice, vegetation, snow cover, water vapor, and other elements of the arctic region.

Students can observe patterns of change and correlate to historical weather and climate data from the NOAA *Climate Data Online* (*CDO*) data repository website (*https://ncdc.noaa. gov/cdo-web*). Other student investigations could include relationships between sea ice and ocean currents, how climate change affects sea ice, and investigations into albedo (reflection) and sea ice with corresponding data from the *NASA Earth Observations* (*NEO*) website (*http://neo.sci.gsfc.nasa.gov*). Additional data provided by *NEO* include graphical models of permafrost, snow cover, and more. As you explore the activities that follow for investigating the hydrosphere, think about other ways you could use real-time data in your classroom.

Tables 8.1 and 8.2 (pp. 199 and 200, respectively) list all digital resources used in this chapter.

REFERENCES

National Snow and Ice Data Center. 2016. Arctic sea ice news and analysis. *https://nsidc.org/ arcticseaicenews.*

U.S. Geological Survey (USGS). *GroundWaterWatch. http://groundwaterwatch.usgs.gov/net/ogwnetwork. asp?ncd=rtn.*

U.S. Geological Survey (USGS). *National water information system. http://waterdata.usgs.gov/nwis/rt.*

CHAPTER 8

HYDROSPHERE

TEACHER NOTES: CATCH THE WAVE!

Learning Goal	Students will use buoy data to determine the relationship between wind speed and wave height.
Disciplinary Core Ideas	• Earth materials and systems • The roles of water in Earth's surface processes
Science and Engineering Practices	• Planning and carrying out investigations • Analyzing and interpreting data
Crosscutting Concepts	• Patterns • Cause and effect: Mechanism and explanation
Background Information	Ocean waves are mechanical waves, formed from the energy of the wind as it moves across the water's surface. Wave size depends on three things: wind speed, wind distance (fetch), and wind duration. Sustained, high winds blowing over long distances produce the highest surface waves. Data for this investigation are from the National Oceanographic and Atmospheric Administration (NOAA) National Data Buoy Center (NDBC) website. The NDBC website provides data for wind speed, but not for wind fetch and wind duration (although those can be estimated).

DATA AND TECHNOLOGY

Online Sources	• NOAA NDBC website: *www. ndbc.noaa*.gov • QR Code: See Table 8.1 (p. 199).	*NOAA Buoy Data* app screenshot
App and Device Sources	*NOAA Buoy Reports* app Platform: iOS	
	NOAA Buoy Data app Platform: iOS	
	Marine Weather app Platform: Android	
	NOAA Buoys Live Marine Weather app Platform: Android	

Source: Engineering Goodness LLC.

The NOAA Buoy Data app screenshot shows:

41025 — Diamond Shoals

Latest Verified Data
Jan 30, 2016, 1:50 PM

TEMPERATURE
Air **47°F**   Water **60°F**

Feels Like   44°F
Dew Point   35°F

WIND		WAVE	
Speed	5.8 kts	Height	4.3 ft
Direction	NNW 340°	Peak Period	9 sec
Gust	7.8 kts	Avg Period	6.8 sec
		Direction	E 91°

DATA AND TECHNOLOGY (continued)	
Technology Notes	Not every buoy provides the information necessary to complete the activity. Some just include wind and weather information; others just show wave or wind information, so this investigation likely will involve searching out a set of buoy stations that fulfill the data need. Depending on the resource used to access it, the data might be available as a map or a list.
About the Data	**Data Sampling:** Teachers should help students determine the geographic location and date and/or time for collecting their data. Sampling could be done at one time or several times in one day (which they could use as data points or to calculate a mean, or average).
	Data Type: Wave height should be reported in feet and wind speed in knots. Both are interval–ratio (measured) data types.
	Data Issues: Buoy distance from shore might be a confounding factor; students can explore this by graphing wind speed versus distance and wave height versus distance. Expect outliers and weaker relationships because of the number of confounding factors.

USING AND ADAPTING THE ACTIVITY	
About the Activity	It is important that students understand that although the data likely will show that wave height is correlated to wind speed, the fetch and wind duration also affect wave height. Asking students to identify outliers and to discuss possible reasons for them will build their understanding of the system.
Scaling Down	To simplify this activity, the data could be collected by the teacher in advance or the site could be projected on a white board for students to collect the data as a class. Alternatively, students could work in pairs, each collecting one or two data points, and then pool data together to work as a large group or class to analyze the collected data.
Scaling Up	For added complexity, show students a video clip of a ship in a storm and pose the question "How does weather affect wave height?" Allow students to brainstorm what variables there would be and what data they would need to collect to conduct their own investigation. Alternatively, students could compare data for air pressure, distance to shore, or other variables, or compare data from the Great Lakes to data for the open ocean. Great sources for downloading data for shoreline locations are surfing websites (for example, *www.surf-forecast.com*) and apps (for example, *Surfline*).

	USING AND ADAPTING THE ACTIVITY *(continued)*
Extending	**Waves:** Waves are essential for surfing! So, what is the science of surfing? To investigate this, make a wave bottle. Fill a used, clear water bottle halfway with blue water (that is, water with added blue food coloring) and the rest with mineral oil. Cap the bottle and gently roll it back and forth to simulate the wave action. **Wave Barriers:** What are wave barriers, and how do they work? Why would you want one if you lived near the ocean? Conduct an engineering project to build and test a wave barrier. **Enrichment Using Data:** Students could explore the relationship by comparing one coast to another, onshore and offshore wind directions, and/or data from buoys different distances from shore. The effect of the duration of wind from the same direction might also be worth exploring for more-advanced students.
	ASSESSMENT NOTES
	There is usually a positive correlation between wind speed and wave height, although fetch and duration also affect wave height. Expect outliers in the data.

Name: _____

STUDENT HANDOUT: CATCH THE WAVE!

Activity Goal	In this activity, you will explore the relationship between wave height and wind speed.
Technology Notes	Collect the data from the National Oceanographic and Atmospheric Administration (NOAA) National Data Buoy Center (NDBC), either through the NOAA website (*www.ndbc.noaa.gov*) or from a marine buoy data app on your device.
Orientation Questions	• Are waves at the beach always the same? • Why are waves at the beach higher some days than others? • When you see movies of ships in storms, why are the waves so high?
Directions	1. Working in pairs, find buoy data for 18 stations that show both wind speed and wave height. As you work through the buoy data, keep in mind that not all buoys provide all data. 2. Add the information from 18 buoys to the Data Table, recording wind speed in knots and wave height in feet. Record all data to one decimal place. 3. For your data analysis, create a scatter plot with your data, and then draw a best-fit trend line. Fill in the units on the *x*-axis and *y*-axis 4. Complete the Analysis Questions, Conclusions, and Reflection Question sections.

DATA ANALYSIS SCATTER PLOT

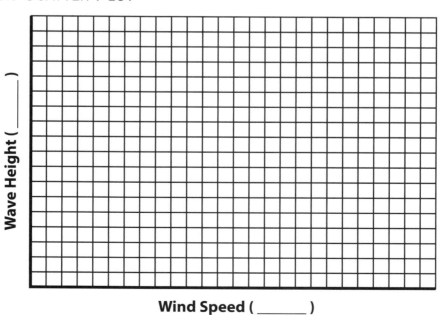

DATA TABLE

Buoy Location	Wind Speed (_____)	Wave Height (_____)

ANALYSIS QUESTIONS

1. Where was your highest wind speed? What was that wind speed, and what was the wave height in this location?

2. Where was your lowest wind speed? What was it and what was the wave height there?

3. What patterns do you notice in the data?

4. Remembering that wave height is affected by three factors—wind speed, wind duration, and fetch—how would you explain the outlying data points?

CONCLUSIONS

What is the relationship between wind speed and wave height? What evidence do you have to support this claim?

REFLECTION QUESTION

How did identifying the pattern help you understand this data?

TEACHER NOTES:
DISSOLVED OXYGEN AND WATER QUALITY

Learning Goal	Students will explore the relationship between water temperature and dissolved oxygen.
Disciplinary Core Ideas	• Natural resources • Earth's systems
Science and Engineering Practices	• Analyzing and interpreting data • Constructing explanations and designing solutions
Crosscutting Concepts	• Energy and matter: Flows, cycles, and conservation • Stability and change
Background Information	Dissolved oxygen in aquatic ecosystems is essential to supporting life and its level in water is a key indicator of water quality. Aeration of moving water increases the dissolved oxygen in a stream, while bacteria thriving on decaying matter or pollution quickly use it up and thus reduce its level. As the level of dissolved oxygen level increases, the diversity of organisms increases and the overall health of the river/stream improves. Water temperature also affects the amount of dissolved oxygen in rivers and streams. Cold water holds more dissolved oxygen, but as water temperature rises, oxygen solubility decreases.

DATA AND TECHNOLOGY		
Online Sources	• U.S. Geological Survey (USGS) *WaterQualityWatch* website: *http:// waterwatch.usgs.gov/wqwatch* • QR Code: See Table 8.1 (p. 199).	USGS *WaterQualityWatch* website screenshot **Real-Time Dissolved Oxygen, in mg/L** February 27, 2015 13:30ET *Source:* U.S. Geological Survey. *http:// waterwatch.usgs.gov/wqwatch.*
App and Device Sources		*River Data Lite* app Platform: iOS
		Water Info USA app Platform: Android

DATA AND TECHNOLOGY *(continued)*	
Technology Notes	When accessing data on the USGS website, select "table" for the output format so that students do not have to try to interpret the values from graphs. The website allows the user to access information for past dates, whereas the apps only allow access current data. Therefore, if the website is used, the focus of an investigation could be limited to a single station over several months, but students using the apps would need to collect data on a single day from multiple sites. Not all sites provide dissolved-oxygen and temperature data; many are limited to gage height and discharge. When using the USGS website, select "Dissolved Oxygen" as the desired measurement before looking at station data. When using the iOS app, look for stations with five or more gauges to locate the desired data.
About the Data	**Data Sampling:** The issues discussed in the Technology Notes section of this activity can cause sampling issues. Also, the rate of water flow (influenced by rainfall) can cause substantial day-to-day changes in levels of dissolved oxygen. Students making comparisons might want to standardize their data based on recent rainfall, or otherwise account for rainfall levels. **Data Type:** Rainfall and dissolved oxygen levels are both interval–ratio data, usually examined using a scatter plot. **Data Issues:** No data issues should arise other from missing data.
USING AND ADAPTING THE ACTIVITY	
About the Activity	The purpose of this activity is for students to see the relationship between water temperature and the levels of dissolved oxygen in rivers and streams. Not all rivers have the same characteristics, and other variables such as streamflow velocity, type and amount of vegetation, and topography will also affect the levels of dissolved oxygen. Ask students to identify outliers and discuss possible variables to help build their understanding of aquatic ecosystems.
Scaling Down	To simplify this activity, students can collect a single data point and share it with other groups to work as a class. Teachers could also collect the data in advance for students to analyze. When using the USGS website, turn off all data except for temperature and dissolved oxygen to avoid confusing students with extraneous data points.
Scaling Up	For added complexity, have students look for other relationships in other variables, for example, precipitation, turbidity, and conductivity. In addition, students can use the USGS *EarthExplorer* website (*http://earthexplorer.usgs.gov*) to find one or more geographic location and identify local topography and other features that can affect water quality.

	USING AND ADAPTING THE ACTIVITY (*continued*)
Extending	**Changes in Multiple Variables:** Using data from the USGS *WaterQualityWatch* website, students can monitor conditions over time to look for changes in multiple variables. They could do this by collecting data from a single site over a long period (for example, monthly for a year) or conduct an in-depth investigation for a short period of time. With these data, students could assess the impact that long-term variations such as drought have at a single station.
	Water Quality and Ecosystem: Another possible activity is to monitor water quality of a single stream as it flows through rural and urban areas.
	Enrichment Using Data: Students might find it useful to graph dissolved oxygen versus rainfall over one year to see patterns over that period. Comparing dissolved oxygen versus temperature on "steep" versus "flat" areas of a river would also reveal interesting patterns.

ASSESSMENT NOTES

Generally, colder water has higher levels of dissolved oxygen. Other factors that might affect levels of dissolved oxygen include topography, flow rate, and the presence of biologic organisms.

Name: _____

STUDENT HANDOUT:
DISSOLVED OXYGEN AND WATER QUALITY

Activity Goal	In this activity, you will explore the relationship between dissolved oxygen and water temperature in streams and rivers.
Technology Notes	Collect the activity data from the U.S. Geological Survey (USGS) *WaterQualityWatch* website (*http://waterwatch.usgs.gov/wqwatch*) or using an app suggested by your teacher.
Orientation Questions	• What is the relationship between dissolved oxygen and water temperature? • Why is dissolved oxygen an important indicator of water quality?
Directions	1. Working in pairs, find dissolved oxygen levels and water temperature data for 15 stream/river stations. As you look through the streamflow station data, remember that not all sites report all types of data. 2. Record the temperature (°C) and dissolved oxygen (mg/L) data in the Data Table. 3. Complete the Data Analysis section by creating a scatter plot to present your data, and then drawing a best-fit trend line. 4. Complete the Analysis Questions, Conclusions, and Reflection Question sections.

DATA ANALYSIS SCATTER PLOT

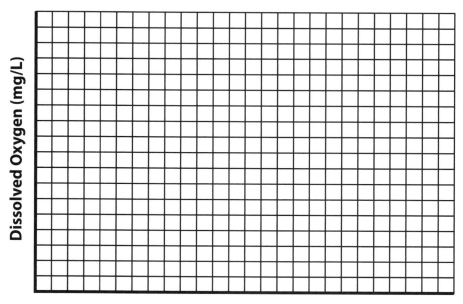

Water Temperature (°C)

DATA TABLE

Location	Water Temperature (°C)	Dissolved Oxygen (mg/L)

ANALYSIS QUESTIONS

1. Is there a relationship between water temperature and dissolved oxygen? Explain, using the trend line to justify your explanation.

2. How would you explain the outliers in the data?

3. What other variables affect dissolved-oxygen levels?

4. Why is dissolved oxygen important for aquatic organisms that live in a stream?

5. Assume that you observe a sudden drop in the level of dissolved oxygen at a particular stream station but no change in water temperature. What possible explanations would account for this sudden change, and what effects could it have on the aquatic organisms living in that stream?

CONCLUSIONS

Construct an explanation that describes the relationship between water temperature and dissolved oxygen. To support your conclusion, cite the evidence you have collected. How do changes in energy (temperature) or matter (rainfall) affect the system?

REFLECTION QUESTION

What seasonal changes would you expect to find at a single station over the course of a year? Explain.

TEACHER NOTES: OCEANS AND CLIMATE

Learning Goal	Students will explore how oceans mitigate climate at midlatitudes.
Disciplinary Core Ideas	• The roles of water in Earth's surface processes • Weather and climate
Science and Engineering Practices	• Developing and using models • Engaging in argument from evidence
Crosscutting Concepts	• Systems and system models • Energy and matter: Flows, cycles, and conservation
Background Information	Oceans affect climate by transporting heat from the equator toward the poles while transporting cool water from the poles toward the equator. The prevailing winds (from the west, at the midlatitudes) are warmed or cooled by the ocean before they pass over land. As an example of this ocean effect on climate, the year-round climate is usually milder for U.S. West Coast cities than for East Coast locations. In the summer, West Coast cities are usually cooler than East Coast cities because the air on the West Coast has been cooled by passing over the cold California Current. But winters on the West Coast are also milder than on the East Coast, because water heats and cools very slowly and during the winter, the Pacific Ocean continues to warm the air that moves over it before passing over land.

DATA AND TECHNOLOGY

Online Sources	• For latitude and longitude, the LatLong website: *www.latlong.net* • For historical climate data, the Weather Underground website: *www.wunderground.com/history* • QR Codes: See Table 8.1 (p. 199).	*Weather History Explorer* app screenshot
App and Device Sources	*Coordinates app* (for latitude and longitude) Platform: iOS	
	Map Coordinates app (for latitude and longitude) Platform: Android	*Source:* Savchenko, V. 2014. *Weather History Explorer* app.
	Weather History Explorer app (for weather history data) Platforms: iOS, Android	

DATA AND TECHNOLOGY (continued)	
Technology Notes	Students will first need to identify cities by latitude, either using the LatLong website or an app, so they then can find cities at similar latitudes. The *Weather History Explorer* app provides much more information than students will need for this activity, but the information students need (mean [average] high and low temperature [°F] for each location) is shown with the green bar near the bottom of the screen (not the blue bar).
About the Data	**Data Sampling:** Teachers might need to help students determine which cities to use so that they are distributed along the entire coast. This allows a fair comparison of the two coasts. **Data Type:** Temperature/temperature range is the "measured" (or interval–ratio) type of data so means can be calculated. **Data Issues:** No data issues anticipated.
USING AND ADAPTING THE ACTIVITY	
About the Activity	In this activity, students will compare climates for east and west coast cities in North America to see how oceans mitigate the climate of locations on the west coast. Students will need to identify cities at both locations at approximately the same latitude with one app or website, and then the mean high and low temperatures for each city with a second app or website. Students should have experience with differential heating and cooling of land and water before completing this investigation.
Scaling Down	To simplify this activity, provide students with a list of cities at similar latitudes (for example, Portland, Maine, and Eugene, Oregon, at 43.6N latitude) and assign them to collect data on individual locations as a jigsaw activity.
Scaling Up	For added complexity, have groups of students collect data at specific latitude bands (for example, 30° to 39°, 40° to 49°, 50° to 59°) and then share their data to compare the variations that occur at different latitudes. Students can plot the data on a scatter plot to determine whether there is relationship between latitude and temperature range in the data collected. They also will see how various cold and warm water currents affect climate.
Extending	**Effects of Other Variables:** Have students collect data for temperature and precipitation for five cities along the same line of latitude across the United States. These data should be plotted on a map, along with geographic features such as mountains. Then students can analyze the collected data to determine other variables, such as topography and effect on climate. **Enrichment Using Data:** There might be considerable variation in the data around the mean range. After students have plotted the bar graph, have them put marks where the "range" for each city would be found and have them incorporate that information into their conclusions.

CHAPTER 8

HYDROSPHERE

ASSESSMENT NOTES

West Coast locations will generally see warmer temperatures in the winter and cooler temperatures in the summer at the midlatitudes because of Pacific Ocean currents influencing air masses. The temperature ranges in East Coast cities are greater than in West Coast cities.

Name: _____

HYDROSPHERE

STUDENT HANDOUT: OCEANS AND CLIMATE

Activity Goal	In this activity, you will explore how oceans interact with prevailing winds to affect climate.
Technology Notes	You will need two sets of information for this investigation. To identify the latitude and longitude of cities, use the LatLong website (*www.latlong. net*). To find climate data, use the Weather Underground website (*www. wunderground.com/history*). Alternatively, your teacher might ask you to use specific apps to find the needed data.
Orientation Questions	• How do oceans affect climate? • How do the climates of East Coast and West Coast cities in the United States differ? • How do global winds and ocean currents interact to influence climate?

Directions	1. Using the LatLong website or an app, identify five pairs of cities at about the same latitude, with one city in each pair located on the East Coast and the other on the West Coast. List the pairs in the data table and plot their approximate position on the map provided.
	
	2. Use the Weather Underground website or an app to find these temperature data for each city
	    a. Mean (average) winter high and low temperatures as of January 10.
	    b. Mean summer high and low temperatures as of July 10.
	
	3. Calculate the range of mean temperatures for each city by subtracting the mean winter low from the mean summer high, and then record it.
	
	4. Calculate the mean temperature range for all cities on each coast.
	
	5. Perform data analysis on these data by constructing a bar graph using the provided graph template.
	
	6. Complete the Analysis Questions, Conclusions, and Reflection Question sections.

DATA TABLE

Latitude	West Coast				East Coast			
		Mean High/Low				Mean High/Low		
Temp = temperature	City and State	Summer Temp (°F)	Winter Temp (°F)	Temp Range	City and State	Summer Temp (°F)	Winter Temp (°F)	Temp Range
Example:								
38° N	Bodega, CA	63/50	54/43	20	Ocean City, MD	84/72	48/30	54
Mean Temperature Range (°F):					Mean Temperature Range (°F):			

MAP

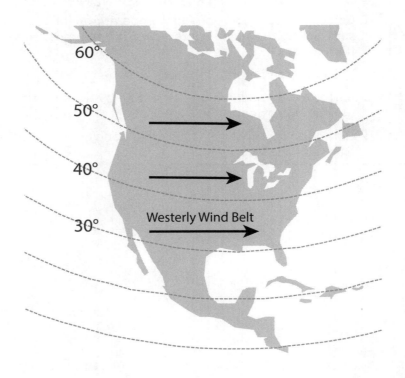

Data Analysis

Construct a bar graph to compare the mean temperature range for East Coast and West Coast cities. Title the graph and label the *y*-axis.

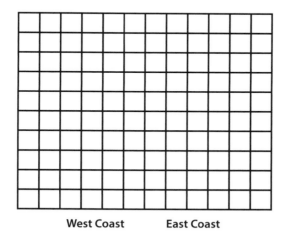

West Coast   East Coast

Analysis Questions

1. Compare the data for East and West Coast cities. Which set of cities had the greatest temperature ranges? Least?

2. Which set of cities had the mildest winters? Mildest summers?

3. What effect does latitude have on the mean summer and winter temperatures?

4. How does latitude affect the range of temperatures?

5. How do you think the climates would change if the winds came from the east?

6. How would the information from the data you collected influence your wardrobe for living on each coast?

Conclusions

Construct an argument that explains how oceans influence climate. Use examples from the data you collected to support your conclusions.

Reflection Question

Compare your data to that of other groups. Do the data collected by other groups support or contradict your observations? Explain.

TEACHER NOTES: TIDES OF CHANGE

Learning Goal	Students will explore the relationship between the ocean tides and the cycles of the Moon.
Disciplinary Core Ideas	• The roles of water in Earth's surface processes • Earth materials and systems
Science and Engineering Practices	• Analyzing and interpreting data • Constructing explanations and designing solutions
Crosscutting Concepts	• Patterns • Cause and effect: Mechanism and explanation
Background Information	Tides are caused by the gravitational pull of the Sun and the Moon. Activities such as shipping, sailing, scuba diving, and fishing are all affected by tides. During the new and full Moons, Earth, the Moon, and the Sun are aligned, and the tug of gravity causes the greatest tidal range. This tidal range is called the "spring tide." During the first quarter and last quarter Moon phases, the Sun and Moon are perpendicular to Earth, pulling Earth's oceans in different directions. During these phases, the tidal range is smaller and referred to as "neap tide." However, coastal topography also helps determine the tidal range for any given location. In some places, such as the Bay of Fundy, Canada, the differences in tidal range are large, whereas other locations, such as the northern Gulf Coast (coasts of Louisiana, Mississippi, and Alabama), see very small differences.

DATA AND TECHNOLOGY		
Online Sources	• U.S. Naval Observatory (USNO) *Phases of the Moon* website: *http://aa.usno.navy.mil/data/docs/MoonPhase.php* • National Oceanic and Atmospheric Administration (NOAA) *Tide Predictions* website: *https://tidesandcurrents.noaa.gov/tide_predictions.html* • QR Codes: See Table 8.1 (p. 199).	NOAA *Tide Predictions* website screenshot **Coffins Point, ME StationId: 8410714** Daily Tide Prediction in Feet 2016/02/27 - 2016/02/28 Time Zone: LST/LDT Datum: MLLW *(graph of predicted tide height)*
App and Device Sources	*Tide Chart Free* app (for Moon phases and Earth tides) Platforms: iOS, Android	*Source:* National Oceanic and Atmospheric Administration. *https://tidesandcurrents.noaa.gov/tide_predictions.html.*

DATA AND TECHNOLOGY (*continued*)	
Technology Notes	If accessing data through a web browser, students will first have to find the Moon phase data on the USNO website, and then find the tide data on the NOAA website. If using the app, students can go to the calendar view for the current month and select the Moon phases from the calendar for different locations. Note that the data are given in feet for all locations in both the app and the NOAA website.
About the Data	**Data Sampling:** No data sampling issues anticipated. It might help students to pick places they have visited or places they would like to go. Students should record tidal height for the same day and Moon phase for each location. **Data Type:** Tide height is interval–ratio data type, and Moon phase is an ordinal (sequential/time) variable in which cycles will be observed. **Data Issues:** Depending on their direction, strong winds can influence tidal height considerably, so there can be considerable variation in measured tides versus anticipated tides.
USING AND ADAPTING THE ACTIVITY	
About the Activity	Students should be careful to choose locations on the coast, not inland. Some locations have only one high and low tide a day (diurnal), whereas others have two (semidiurnal), and still others have a tidal pattern of one tide greater than the second each day (mixed). For locations with mixed, semidiurnal tides, have students collect data for the greater of the tides.
Scaling Down	To simplify this activity, identify specific locations for which you want student to collect data, and pull up their tidal charts. Project or print the tidal charts and have students work from them, instead of finding the tide information in the app or on the website.
Scaling Up	For added complexity, ask students to work in groups, with each group concentrating on a specific coastal location (for example, Gulf, Atlantic, Pacific). Then, map and compare the data from each group. Have students compare tidal patterns (diurnal, semidiurnal, or mixed). Using the website, rather than the app, pull tidal charts for specific locations and have students predict the phase of the Moon.

USING AND ADAPTING THE ACTIVITY (*continued*)	
Extending	**Tidal Data:** Have students collect tidal data over a period of several days and then trade data with each other. Students then could graph the data they received to create their own charts. **Tides as Energy:** Research how tides can be used as a source of energy for power plants. **Patterns in Time:** Have students explore patterns in time and identify the time span between consecutive high and low tides. **Coastal Topography Effects:** Explore how coastal topography affects tides. **Enrichment Using Data:** More-advanced students can do a comparison between predicted and measured tide height and relate these to wind direction and shoreline features.

ASSESSMENT NOTES
Student data should show greater tidal ranges during the full and new Moons (spring tide) and smaller ranges during the quarter phases (neap tide). Different locations may have greater differences in overall tidal ranges, depending on coastal topography.

Name: _____ HYDROSPHERE

STUDENT HANDOUT: TIDES OF CHANGE

Activity Goal	In this activity, you will explore the relationship between the phases of the Moon and the oceans of Earth to explore the role of gravity in tidal patterns.
Technology Notes	• For Moon-phase data, use the U.S. Naval Observatory (USNO) *Phases of the Moon* website: *http://aa.usno.navy.mil/data/docs/MoonPhase.php* • For tide data, use the National Oceanic and Atmospheric Administration (NOAA) *Tide Predictions* website: *https://tidesandcurrents.noaa.gov/tide_predictions.html*
Orientation Questions	• How do the phases of the Moon affect ocean tides? • Are ocean tides the same everywhere?
Directions	1. Using the USNO website or the calendar function in the app, determine the upcoming dates for each phase of the Moon and record these in the data table provided in this activity. 2. Identify three coastal locations that are on different coasts (for example, Pacific, Atlantic, Gulf) or that fit other specific directions from your teacher. 3. Find the high and low tide heights for each date at each location. 4. Determine the tidal range by subtracting the low tide from high tide. 5. Compare locations by summarizing information in the location chart. 6. Use the graph in the Data Analysis section to construct a line graph for the data you collected. 7. Complete the Analysis Questions, Conclusions, and Reflections Questions sections.

DATA TABLE

Moon Phase	Date	Location		High Tide Height (ft)	Low Tide Height (ft)	Tidal Range (ft)
New Moon		1				
		2				
		3				
First Quarter		1				
		2				
		3				
Full Moon		1				
		2				
		3				
Last Quarter		1				
		2				
		3				

DATA ANALYSIS

Construct a line graph showing how the tides change for each location over the course of the lunar month. Graph each location using a different color. Determine the scale (in feet) for the *y*-axis based on your data and label the intervals.

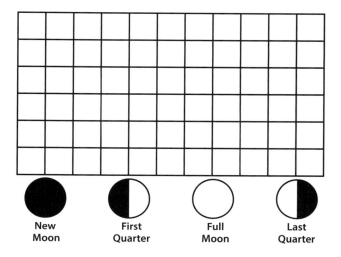

ANALYSIS QUESTIONS

1. During which phase of the Moon are the tides the highest?

2. During which phase of the Moon are the tides the lowest?

3. Which location had the greatest range between high tide and low tide?

4. Which location had the lowest range between high tide and low tide?

5. What patterns did you observe?

6. Were the patterns the same for all three locations? Explain.

7. How would Earth be different if we had no moon? What other than Earth's oceans would be affected?

CONCLUSIONS

When scientists determine a causal relationship, they propose a mechanism to explain the cause. Write an explanation for observed variations in the tidal patterns that describes the role of gravity as the mechanism in producing Earth's tides.

REFLECTION QUESTIONS

What is the difference between correlation and causality? Does correlation necessarily indicate causation?

Table 8.1. Data sources for real-time hydrosphere investigations

Activity	Website	URL	QR Code
Catch the Wave!	NOAA National Data Buoy Center	www.ndbc.noaa.gov	
Dissolved Oxygen and Water Quality	USGS *WaterQualityWatch*	http://waterwatch.usgs.gov/wqwatch	
Oceans and Climate	LatLong	www.latlong.net	
	Weather Underground	www.wunderground.com/history	
Tides of Change	NOAA *Tide Predictions*	https://tidesandcurrents.noaa.gov/tide_predictions.html	
	USNO *Phases of the Moon*	http://aa.usno.navy.mil/data/docs/MoonPhase.php	

Table 8.2. Other sources for hydrosphere data

Website	Address	QR Codes
NOAA *nowCOAST*	*http://nowcoast.noaa.gov*	
USGS *Groundwater Watch*	*http://groundwaterwatch.usgs.gov/net/ogwnetwork. asp?ncd=rtn*	
USGS Daily Streamflow Conditions (Figure 8.1)	*http://waterdata.usgs.gov/nwis/rt*	

INVESTIGATIONS USING REAL-TIME CELESTIAL SPHERE DATA

Data sets that deal with Earth's place in the universe include solar and lunar phenomena, celestial events, satellite orbits, and more. Phenomena such as sunset and sunrise times, Moon phases, planetary transits, incoming solar radiation, and fluctuations in Earth's magnetic field are important to all Earth's systems. They are observed with instruments on Earth's surface and from satellites orbiting our planet.

The U.S. Naval Observatory (USNO) website (*www.usno.navy.mil/USNO*) is the best source of data for sunrise and sunset times; Moon phases; azimuth and altitude positions of celestial objects, including the Sun and the Moon; and much more. There are many investigations students could perform using data from the *USNO* website. For example, students could explore seasonal variations in photoperiods at the location of their home, or compare sunrise and sunset data for locations at different latitudes on any given day. The azimuth and altitude of the Sun and the Moon can help students understand insolation (energy received from the Sun) and seasons.

As an example, Table 9.1 (p. 202) contains monthly data for the Sun's altitude over the period of one year. The 21st day of each month was chosen because it corresponds most closely with the solstices and equinoxes. The altitude data shows the angular height of the Sun above the horizon. To better understand the data, picture the sky as 360°—a circle with its edges along its horizon. The altitude is how far above the horizon an object appears, given in degrees, with 90° being at the zenith, or the point over your head. Analyzing these data or constructing a model to illustrate the monthly differences would help students see how incoming solar radiation changes during the course of the year because of seasonal changes in insolation.

The USNO website also provides azimuthal data that helps students track objects in the sky. Azimuth is the angle from north on the horizon, in degrees. Finding azimuth is like using a compass, with 0° and 360° due north, 90° east, 180° south, and 270° west. Knowing both the altitude and azimuth of a celestial body will allow students to find objects in the sky in real time.

The *NASA Earth Observations* (*NEO*) website (*http://neo.sci.gsfc.nasa.gov*) provides graphic data of energy in Earth's systems, including incoming solar radiation, ultraviolet radiation,

Table 9.1. Solar altitude of the Sun at noon in Chicago, Illinois

Date	Altitude
January 21	28.3°
February 21	37.7°
March 21 (spring equinox)	46.5°
April 21	58.2°
May 21	66.2°
June 21 (summer solstice)	68.6°
July 21	65.4°
August 21	58.0°
September 21 (fall equinox)	47.6°
October 21	36.8°
November 21	28.0°
December 21 (winter solstice)	24.7°

Source: U.S. Naval Observatory. http://aa.usno.navy.mil/data/docs/AltAz.php.

land and sea surface temperatures, and outgoing longwave radiation. These images can be used to explore seasonal variations, compare data trends over the last decade, and support investigations using data from other sources. For example, when investigating the differences in insolation using solar altitude referred to in Table 9.1, students can view the images provided to visualize how incoming solar energy changes as the angle of the Sun increases and decreases.

On its Human Space Flight Realtime Data website (*http://spaceflight.nasa.gov/realdata*), NASA also provides real-time data for tracking satellites. A nongovernment website, FlightAware (*https://flightaware.com/live*), allows tracking and information about current air traffic. Students can monitor the flight paths of satellites to better understand how data are collected, and monitor air plane traffic to better understand the curvature of Earth's surface. The activities that follow provide examples of how to use these data.

Tables 9.2 and 9.3 (pp. 224 and 226, respectively), list all digital resources used in this chapter.

REFERENCE

U.S. Naval Observatory (USNO). *USNO Sun or Moon Altitude/Azimuth Table. http://aa.usno.navy.mil/data/docs/AltAz.php.*

TEACHER NOTES: PHOTOPERIODS

Learning Goal	Students will see how photoperiods change during a year, at locations at different latitudes.
Disciplinary Core Ideas	• Earth and the solar system • Earth's systems
Science and Engineering Practices	• Analyzing and interpreting data • Constructing explanations and designing solutions
Crosscutting Concepts	• Energy and matter: Flows, cycles, and conservation • Stability and change
Background Information	Seasons on Earth are a result of Earth's axial tilt as it orbits the Sun. In the summer, the hemisphere facing the Sun has longer days and receives more direct sunlight. In the winter, the days are shorter. The length of the day varies through the year because the Sun's path across the sky lengthens in the summer and shortens in the winter. At the equator, days are nearly always 12 hours long; however, as you move away from the equator toward the pole, summer-month photoperiods lengthen and winter-month photoperiods shorten. The U.S. Naval Observatory (USNO) maintains precise data from tracking the seasonal changes in photoperiods and the path of the Sun and the Moon as they move across the sky. Students will access these data to compare the changes in photoperiods through seasons at different latitudes.

DATA AND TECHNOLOGY

| Online Sources | • USNO *Complete Sun and Moon Data for One Day* website: *http://aa.usno.navy.mil/data/docs/RS_OneDay.php*
• QR Code: See Table 9.2 (p. 224). | USNO website screenshot

Sun and Moon Data for One Day

U.S. Naval Observatory
Astronomical Applications Department

New York, NY (Longitude W73° 55', Latitude N40° 44')

Tuesday, June 21, 2016 — Eastern Daylight Time

Sun
Begin civil twilight — 4:51 a.m.
Sunrise — 5:25 a.m.
Sun transit — 12:58 p.m.
Sunset — 8:30 p.m.
End civil twilight — 9:04 p.m.

Moon
Moonrise — 8:33 p.m. on preceding day
Moon transit — 1:35 a.m.
Moonset — 6:39 a.m.
Moonrise — 9:22 p.m.

Source: U.S. Naval Observatory. *http://aa.usno.navy.mil/data/docs/RS_OneDay.php.* |
| App and Device Sources | *Sun Rise and Fall* app
Platform: iOS

Sunrise Sunset app
Platform: Android | |

DATA AND TECHNOLOGY (*continued*)	
Technology Notes	The USNO website has a responsive design and will work on small devices. The *Sun Rise and Fall* app calculates and shows the "Sun Up" time, and for this reason is better for students who might have difficulty calculating the photoperiods from sunrise and sunset times. Both apps require students to drop or move the "pin," whereas the USNO website requires students to enter in location names. On the website, students will need to use Form A for locations in the United States and Form B for locations outside the United States.
About the Data	**Data Sampling:** No sampling issues anticipated. **Data Type:** The data for comparison are the interval–ratio data type (that is, dates), but the data points for photoperiod-length points representing June 21–September 21–December 21 will be joined, essentially making the categories the ordinal (that is, ordered category) data type. **Data Issues:** The scatter plot in this activity is a more complex type, with a nonlinear line of best fit. Students might benefit from being shown a rough model of what it will look like. Students might also want to convert the photoperiod's hours:minutes to total minutes. **Enrichment Using Data:** Students might find it interesting to create a sequential *x-y* graph of photoperiod length versus day of the year so they can see how the photoperiod varies cyclically over the span of a year.

USING AND ADAPTING THE ACTIVITY	
About the Activity	The most difficult part of this activity for students is to calculate the photoperiod from the sunrise and sunset times. First, they will need to convert these times to military time, because we have a 24-hour day but use a 12-hour clock. When subtracting the sunrise time from the sunset time, students must borrow from hours to minutes in six, 10-minute blocks, not the normal base-10 borrowing. Geography skills also can be a problem, and it would help for students to have maps and globes for reference.
Scaling Down	To simplify this activity, have students in different groups collect different data. To work with less data, students might only collect solstice data to compare the longest and shortest days or might compare fewer locations. Mathematical shortcuts can be used; for example, using a time calculator such as the one on the Timeanddate.com *Date and Time Calculator* website (*www.timeanddate.com/date/timeadd.html*).

USING AND ADAPTING THE ACTIVITY *(continued)*	
Scaling Up	For added complexity, have students work in teams, with different groups collecting data for the equinox and the winter solstice for comparison. Allow students to use cities of their own choosing at different latitudes rather than the cities on the handout. Students can research some of the cities at similar latitudes to see how their climates vary based on other factors, such as precipitation and ocean currents.
Extending	**Photoperiods Over a Year:** Explore how photoperiods change over the year using the *Earth and Moon Viewer* website (*https://fourmilab.ch/cgi-bin/Earth/action?opt=-p*). **Photoperiods "Mystery Class":** Participate in the *Journey North* website "Mystery Class" project (*www.learner.org/jnorth/mclass*), in which classes identify locations based on photoperiods and clues. **Photoperiods and Plants:** How does photoperiod length affect plants? Research short-day and long-day plants to see how life responds to photoperiods.

ASSESSMENT NOTES
At the equator, days are nearly always 12 hours long; however, as you move away from the equator toward the pole, summer-month photoperiods lengthen and winter-month photoperiods shorten.

Name: _____

STUDENT HANDOUT: PHOTOPERIODS

Activity Goal	In this activity, you will collect data about the sunrise and sunset times at different latitudes to identify seasonal changes in photoperiods.
Technology Notes	The U.S. Naval Observatory (USNO) *Complete Sun and Moon Data for One Day* website maintains precise sunrise and sunset data for all locations. Access these data at *http://aa.usno.navy.mil/data/docs/ RS_OneDay.php* or by using an app suggested by your teacher.
Orientation Questions	• How does the length of the day vary among different locations? • How do photoperiods change during different seasons? • Where would you go to see the Sun be up for 24 hours a day in the summer?
Directions	1. Using the *USNO* website, find the sunrise and sunset times for the city you live in on each of the dates shown in Data Table 1. Record the location, latitude, and times in that data table. Show north latitude as positive (+) and south latitude as negative (−). 2. Calculate the photoperiod by subtracting the sunrise time from the sunset time. Before subtracting, you must convert the sunset time to military time by adding 12 hours to it. 3. Find the sunrise and sunset times for all locations in Data Table 2 on June 21—the summer solstice—and record them. 4. Calculate and record the photoperiod in hours and minutes for each location. 5. Complete the Data Analysis section by constructing a scatter plot to show the relationship between latitude and photoperiod on the summer solstice (June 21). Then, draw a trend line. 6. Complete the Analysis Questions, Conclusions, and Reflection Question sections.

CELESTIAL SPHERE

DATA TABLE 1. PHOTOPERIODS FOR DIFFERENT SEASONS AT STUDENT'S LOCATION

Location	Latitude	Date	Sunrise Time	Sunset Time	Photoperiod
		June 21			
		September 21			
		December 21			

DATA TABLE 2. SUMMER SOLSTICE (JUNE 21) PHOTOPERIODS AT DIFFERENT LOCATIONS

Location	Latitude	Sunrise Time	Sunset Time	Photoperiod
Pensacola, Florida (United States)	+30 (N)			
Paris, France (Europe)	+49 (N)			
Fairbanks, Alaska (United States)	+65 (N)			
Nairobi, Kenya (Africa)	−2 (S)			
Sydney, Australia	−33 (S)			
Queenstown, New Zealand	−45 (S)			
Punta Arenas, Chile (South America)	−53 (S)			

DATA ANALYSIS SCATTER PLOT

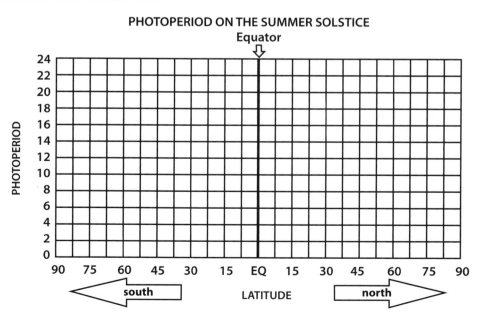

Analysis Questions

1. How different are the photoperiods at different seasons where you live? What date was the longest? The shortest? How much difference was there between them?

2. What is the relationship between latitude and photoperiod on the summer solstice?

3. Which location in Data Table 2 has a June 21 photoperiod closest to the photoperiod where you live? What city has the closest latitude to your location's?

4. In what ways do you think photoperiods are different in the winter? Collect some additional data for cities both north and south of the equator on the winter solstice (December 21) to test your hypothesis, and then explain what you discovered.

5. In what ways do you think photoperiods are different in the spring and fall? Collect some additional data for cities both north and south of the equator on the equinox (March/ September 21) to test your hypothesis, and then explain what you discovered.

Conclusions

Based on what you know about Earth's tilt on its axis, create a model (for example, an annotated illustration) that describes why days are longer in the north during the summer.

Reflection Question

How does the amount of incoming solar energy in each location vary over a year because of the seasonal changes in the photoperiod?

TEACHER NOTES: SOLAR TERMINATOR

Learning Goal	Students will illustrate and compare the patterns of day and night across the globe during different seasons.
Disciplinary Core Ideas	• Earth and the solar system • Earth's systems
Science and Engineering Practices	• Developing and using models • Constructing explanations and designing solutions
Crosscutting Concepts	• Patterns • Energy and matter: Flows, cycles, and conservation
Background Information	Seasonal changes on Earth include not only temperature and precipitation variations, but also changes in the amount of sunlight each day. Days are much longer during the summer than during the winter. The view of Earth from space show that because Earth tilts on its axis, the part of the planet that is receiving sunlight during the day varies according to location and season. During the equinoxes, the solar terminator (the line between day and night) is vertical, whereas on the solstices, it is curved toward the pole. Viewing the changes of the solar terminator across seasons can help students to better understand seasonal changes in solar energy on Earth.

DATA AND TECHNOLOGY		

Online Sources	• U.S. Naval Observatory (USNO) *Day and Night Across the Earth* website: *http://aa.usno.navy.mil/data/docs/earthview.php* • Timeanddate.com *Day and Night World Map* website: *http://timeanddate.com/worldclock/sunearth.html?iso=20161221T1044&n=25* • QR Codes: See Table 9.2 (p. 224).	USNO website screenshot U.S. Naval Observatory Astronomical Applications Department **Illumination map of Earth at March 6, 2016 21:01 UT** *Source :* U.S. Naval Observatory. *http://aa.usno.navy.mil/data/docs/earthview.php.*
App and Device Sources		*Day & Night Map* app Platforms: iOS, Android

DATA AND TECHNOLOGY *(continued)*	
Technology Notes	The USNO website has a responsive design and will work well on small devices. However, it does not illustrate the current position of the Sun. The graphics produced on the Timeanddate.com website and *Day & Night Map* app include the current position of the Sun. The app uses a slider bar or calendar to select the date and time.
About the Data	**Data Sampling:** No sampling issues anticipated. **Data Type:** The data for most comparisons are the nominal (that is, unordered category) data type. Distance values are given in millimeters (mm). **Data Issues:** Measurements made on a larger screen size might not fit on the graph. In that case, either use larger graph paper or a divisor to reduce all values to fit on the provided graph.
USING AND ADAPTING THE ACTIVITY	
About the Activity	The view produced on both the app and the website is centered on the prime meridian. Students should understand that the map projection is a distorted view and that Earth is spherical. The USNO website allows students to see the spherical view as an alternate; however, the graphic produced does not allow for manipulation.
Scaling Down	To simplify this activity, take screenshots for easy comparison rather than having students illustrate each view.
Scaling Up	For added complexity, add a Moon-phase correlation. The TimeandDate.com website and *Day & Night Map* app both show the positions of the Moon and the Sun. Students can use their relative positions to predict the phase of the Moon for each date, and then verify using a Moon-phase app or the USNO *Phases of the Moon* website (*http://aa.usno.navy.mil/data/docs/MoonPhase.php*).

	USING AND ADAPTING THE ACTIVITY *(continued)*
Extending	**Image Processing:** By calibrating the images with known distances, students can measure the distance between the Sun's northernmost and southernmost positions on the solstices. For this activity, students can work with "Image J" software— free, downloadable software for processing screenshots, available from the National Institutes of Health website (*http://imagej.nih.gov/ij*) **Lahaina Noon:** In Hawaii, Lahaina Noon is the time of year when the Sun passes directly overhead. This happens twice a year—once as the Sun journeys north and again on its way south. Have students research on what dates these occur, and then view those dates on the TimeandDate.com website or an app. They can then use the TimeandDate.com website to identify other dates and locations of the Sun at its zenith, and mark those locations on the map.

ASSESSMENT NOTES

A clear pattern should be evident. On the equinoxes, the terminator lines should be nearly parallel, north to south. On the solstices, the terminator should curve with the North Pole being entirely in daylight during the (Northern Hemisphere) summer and the South Pole being in total daylight during the (Northern Hemisphere) winter. Check to see that student measurements are reasonable, being nearly the same length during solstices and progressing differences during solstices.

CELESTIAL SPHERE

Name: _____

STUDENT HANDOUT: SOLAR TERMINATOR

Activity Goal	In this activity, you will construct a visual model of the seasonal differences in the amount of daylight in locations across the globe.
Technology Notes	Access the needed data at the TimeandDate.com website (*http:// timeanddate.com/worldclock/sunearth.html?iso=20161221T1044&n=25*) or using an app recommended by your teacher.
Orientation Questions	• What do seasonal changes on Earth look like from space? • How does the part of Earth in sunlight on the winter solstice compare with the sunlit part on the summer solstice?
Directions	1. Using the website or an app, look up the view of Earth on today's date at noon. 2. On the top left map of the Map Set provided, shade in the part of Earth that now is in night. Also mark the Sun's current position with a sun symbol. 3. Change the date to noon on June 21 for the summer solstice view, either September 21 or March 21 for the equinox view, and December 21 for the winter solstice view. 4. For each date, shade in each map to show the part of Earth that is in night, and show the position of the Sun. 5. Using a metric ruler, measure the distance in millimeters between the eastern and western solar terminator (the line that marks where day and night meet) for the daylight section at the northernmost and southernmost positions. Record that information on the data table. 6. Complete the Data Analysis section by constructing a double bar graph to show the difference in distance (in mm) at the solar terminator for the northernmost and southernmost positions at each season. 7. Complete the Analysis Questions, Conclusions, and Reflection Question sections.

NATIONAL SCIENCE TEACHERS ASSOCIATION

MAP SET

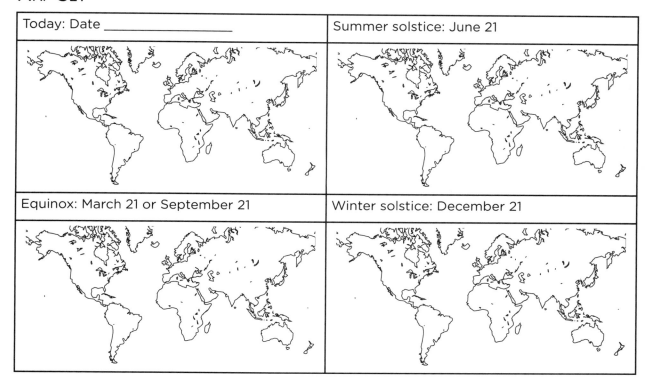

| Today: Date _____ | Summer solstice: June 21 |
| Equinox: March 21 or September 21 | Winter solstice: December 21 |

DATA TABLE

Time of Year	Northern Solar Terminator Distance (mm)	Southern Solar Terminator Distance (mm)
Today: Date _____		
Summer solstice		
Equinox		
Winter solstice		

DATA ANALYSIS

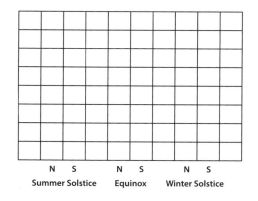

CHAPTER 9

Analysis Questions

1. What is the shape of the solar terminator on Earth during the summer and winter? How does this compare with its shape on the equinox shape?

2. Is the Sun ever straight over your head where you live? If so, when? If not, what is the closest it gets, and when?

3. What does the change in the Sun's position at different seasons suggest about the amount of incoming solar energy at different latitudes?

4. The distance you measured between terminators represents the length of the shortest and longest day for each season at a particular latitude. During summer, how does day length compare in the northern and southern hemispheres? During winter?

5. What does the pattern observed on the equinox suggest about the length of the day in different locations on Earth?

Conclusions

Use what you know about how Earth tilts on its axis to construct an explanation for why the solar terminator is curved.

Reflection Question

How do the images you collected model the seasonal changes in sunlight at different latitudes during the year?

TEACHER NOTES: TONIGHT'S SKY

Learning Goal	In this activity, students will discover what planets they can locate in the evening sky and where to find them.
Disciplinary Core Ideas	• Earth's place in the universe
Science and Engineering Practices	• Analyzing and interpreting data • Constructing explanations and designing solutions
Crosscutting Concepts	• System and system models • Stability and change
Background Information	As planets in the solar system orbit the Sun, their position changes relative to the background of stars, which appear to be locked in position within their designated constellation. Scientists use local coordinates (azimuth, altitude) to specify a planet's position relative to the Earth's surface as it moves across the sky; however, scientists use a different coordinate system—right ascension (RA) and declination (Dec.)—to indicate the fixed position of stars on the celestial sphere, that is, their position relative to each other. Right ascension is the equivalent of longitude on Earth's surface, running pole to pole. Declination is the terrestrial equivalent of latitude, indicating the position of a star above or below the celestial equator. A planet's RA and declination will reveal its current position relative to its background of stars.

DATA AND TECHNOLOGY	
Online Sources	• U.S. Naval Observatory (USNO) *Topocentric Configuration of Major Solar System Bodies* website: *http://aa.usno.navy.mil/data/docs/ssconf.php* • USNO *Rise/Set/Transit Times for Major Solar System Bodies and Bright Stars* website: *http://aa.usno.navy.mil/data/docs/mrst.php* • QR Codes: See Table 9.2 (p. 224).	USNO *Topocentric Configuration of Major Solar System Bodies* website screenshot: *Source:* U.S. Naval Observatory. *http://aa.usno.navy.mil/data/docs/ssconf.php.*
App and Device Sources	Apps are available, but most are costly.	

DATA AND TECHNOLOGY *(continued)*	
Technology Notes	When accessing data on the USNO website you will use the Form A for U.S. locations and Form B for non-U.S. locations. The website has a responsive design and works well on small devices.
About the Data	**Data Sampling:** Data sampling will be relatively straightforward, because students are collecting current-position data using celestial coordinates and rise and set times. **Data Type:** The location data is nominal (the planet positions are all independent from each other); however, instead of graphing, students will be locating the position of the planets on a "map" of the celestial sphere. **Data Issues:** Retrograde motion for planets can result in unexpected differences between two dates.

USING AND ADAPTING THE ACTIVITY	
About the Activity	In this activity, students will identify the current position of planets along the ecliptic. Students should have an understanding that the ecliptic is an extension of Earth's orbital path around the Sun, which all planets stay near as they orbit the Sun, and that the zodiac constellations are the constellations through which the ecliptic passes. Using data for the current position and the rise and set times for the Sun, the Moon, and each of the five naked-eye planets, students can determine when and where to look for each of these planets in the night sky. Students who struggle with latitude and longitude might have problems with plotting RA and declination and will need group practice before working individually.
Scaling Down	To simplify this activity, have students work in pairs or small groups to find the information for a single planet, then work as a large group to plot the positions of the planets on a class chart. Alternatively, students can use sky maps such as are on the Lunaf website (*http://lunaf.com/space/ sky-map*) and the Sky Marvels website (*www.skymarvels.com/infopages/ solarsysteminfo.htm*) to find the location of each planet in the zodiac constellations without using RA or declination. With this method, students must view sky maps from different continents to see the full ecliptic.
Scaling Up	For added complexity, students can use the change in celestial motion over the 30-day period to hypothesize about where each planet will be after a year. Then, they can use the topocentric data from the USNO *Topocentric Configuration of Major Solar System Bodies* website to check the closeness of their predictions. Another option would be to focus on the daily movement of the Moon over one month. How does its movement compare with that of the planets?

USING AND ADAPTING THE ACTIVITY *(continued)*	
Extending	**Star party!** Borrow some binoculars or telescopes or invite a local astronomy club to hold a star party. Have students locate the visible planets within each constellation along the ecliptic. **What's my zodiac sign?** Have students determine where the planets will be on their birthday. They could draw a star chart indicating the position of the Sun and planets on their special day, as well as figure out their zodiac sign. **Enrichment Using Data:** Students can work with local coordinates (azimuth, zenith distance), apparent magnitude, and other information provided with the topocentric data to explore patterns over time while the planets orbit the Sun.

ASSESSMENT NOTES
When plotting the current position of each planet, declination should put the planets near the ecliptic. Venus and Mercury will always be near the Sun. Celestial bodies that are closest to Earth will generally move the most across the sky over the 15-day period; however, planets that are moving retrograde (apparent reverse motion) might not appear to move much at all, or might appear to move backward, and could affect any assertions students make.

Student Name: _____

STUDENT HANDOUT: TONIGHT'S SKY

Activity Goal	In this activity, you will identify the current location in the sky of each of the naked-eye planets, and identify when and where you can view them.
Technology Notes	Collect the data for this activity from two U.S. Naval Observatory (USNO) websites: *USNO Topocentric Configuration of Major Solar System Bodies* (*http://aa.usno.navy.mil/data/docs/ssconf.php*) and *USNO Rise/Set/ Transit Times for Major Solar System Bodies and Bright Stars* (*http:// aa.usno.navy.mil/data/docs/mrst.php*).
Orientation Questions	• Which planets can you see in tonight's sky? • What does the change in a celestial body's position over time tell you about its relative distance from Earth?
Directions	1. On the USNO topocentric configuration website, complete Form A, indicating your location (city, state) and estimating its altitude (height above sea level) in meters. Set it for a 15-day interval with two iterations. Record the right ascension (RA) and declination (Dec.) for the Sun, the Moon, and the naked-eye planets in the Data Table for the current data and the data for 15 days from now. 2. On the USNO rise/set/transit times website, complete Form A as you did in the previous step. Select the Sun, the Moon and each naked-eye planet separately. Record the rise and set time for each planet. 3. Chart the current location of each celestial body on the Sky Chart. 4. Complete the Analysis Questions, Conclusions, and Reflection Question sections.

ANALYSIS QUESTIONS

1. Which planets will be visible after dark tonight?

2. Why are the planets that rise during the day not visible in the sky?

3. Which celestial object moves the most over a 15-day interval?

4. Which celestial object moves the least over a 15-day interval?

CONCLUSIONS

What inference can you make about the change in a celestial body's position over time and its relative distance from Earth?

REFLECTION QUESTION

How would retrograde motion affect the movement of a planet across the sky over time?

DATA TABLE

Sun			
Tonight's data			
Rise time		Set time	
RA		Dec.	
15-day data			
RA		Dec.	

Venus			
Tonight's data			
Rise time		Set time	
RA		Dec.	
15-day data			
RA		Dec.	

Jupiter			
Tonight's data			
Rise time		Set time	
RA		Dec.	
15-day data			
RA		Dec.	

Moon			
Tonight's data			
Rise time		Set time	
RA		Dec.	
15-day data			
RA		Dec.	

Mercury			
Tonight's data			
Rise time		Set time	
RA		Dec.	
15-day data			
RA		Dec.	

Mars			
Tonight's data			
Rise time		Set time	
RA		Dec.	
15-day data			
RA		Dec.	

Saturn			
Tonight's data			
Rise time		Set time	
RA		Dec.	
15-day data			
RA		Dec.	

RA = right ascension; Dec. = declination

CHAPTER 9

CELESTIAL SPHERE

SKY CHART

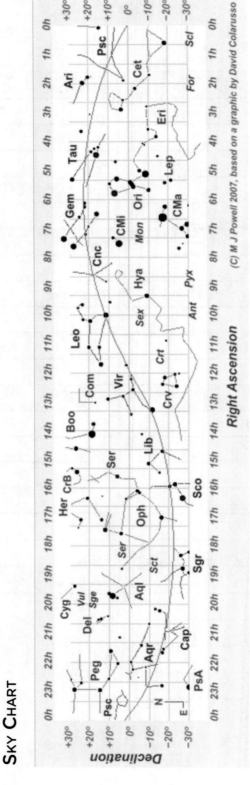

Source: Martin J. Powell (*www.nakedeyeplanets.com*) and David Colarusso (*www.davidcolarusso.com/astro*). Used with permission.

(C) M J Powell 2007, based on a graphic by David Colarusso

TEACHER NOTES: HIDING OUT

Learning Goal	Students will examine the biotic and abiotic features necessary for survival of an organism by developing a plan to go into hiding for a year in a remote place that would provide the conditions to support life. There is no student handout for this activity.
Disciplinary Core Ideas	• Weather and climate • Natural resources
Science and Engineering Practices	• Planning and carrying out investigations • Engaging in argument from evidence
Crosscutting Concepts	• Energy and matter: Flows, cycles, and conservation • Stability and change
Background Information	Animal organisms need to find places to live that allow them to avoid predators, find shelter, and obtain adequate water and nutrition daily. In this exercise, students will consider where they could go and what they would need to "escape humanity" for a year (as a group of 10) and survive. The starting point is using a map of airline flight patterns over the mainland United States to determine areas where they (and any indicators of their existence) could best remain out of sight of a plane (which is an analogue to a predator). Then, they will construct an argument about meeting the other necessities in Maslow's hierarchy of needs.

DATA AND TECHNOLOGY	
Online Sources	**Relevant websites:** • FlightAware: *https://flightaware.com/live* • U.S. Department of Agriculture (USDA) *VegScape Vegetation Condition Explorer*: *https://nassgeodata.gmu.edu/VegScape* • USDA *County Maps*: *www.nass.usda.gov/Charts_and_Maps/Crops_County* • U.S. Naval Observatory (USNO) *Complete Sun and Moon Data for One Day*: *http://aa.usno.navy.mil/data/docs/RS_OneDay.php* • U.S. Geological Survey (USGS) *WaterQualityWatch*: *http://waterwatch.usgs.gov/wqwatch* • National Oceanic and Atmospheric Administration (NOAA) *Tide Predictions*: *https://tidesandcurrents.noaa.gov/tide_predictions.html*

DATA AND TECHNOLOGY *(continued)*	
Online Sources *(continued)*	• Weather Underground *Historical Weather*: www.wunderground.com/history • NOAA National Weather Service: *www.weather.gov* • NOAA *Storm Events Database*: www.ncdc.noaa.gov/stormevents • QR Codes: See Table 9.2 (p. 224).
App and Device Sources	*FlightAware* app Platforms: iOS, Android
	Other relevant apps are also available.
Technology Notes	This open-ended project asks students to think about what data they need, then choose the websites and/or apps to find those data. Some of the websites listed have a responsive design, and most have an app alternative. Technology issues will vary, depending on the sites and/or apps students choose. The teacher might challenge students to share useful apps that can be applied to new investigations.
About the Data	Students will be expected to support and defend their argument using data and graphs about relevant factors, for example, weather patterns, water availability, and the ability to grow crops.
USING AND ADAPTING THE ACTIVITY	
About the Activity	This activity is designed to allow students significant freedom in their explorations (Tamir, Level 3; see Table 3.1, p. 28). It is a very open-ended activity in which students are expected to accumulate an array of resources (including data from various government and nongovernment websites) that they will then use to construct an argument about the best location for a group of 10 of them to hide away and be unfindable for at least a year. The teacher can establish a list of items they might take with them, but the students must attend to the various things that humans need to survive and must determine the best remote spot in the United States where all of their survival and secrecy needs will be met. It is possible that people will be looking for them, so they must choose a spot away from both roads and planes flying overhead (as per the flight tracking website or app). Teachers might want to create a rubric with specific criteria, or they might have students help establish guidelines and construct a rubric for project evaluation.
Scaling Down	To simplify this activity, shorten the list of needs students must meet, expand the list of resources they can take with them, and decrease the size of the groups.

USING AND ADAPTING THE ACTIVITY (*continued*)	
Scaling Up	For added complexity, lengthen the list of needs students must meet, lengthen their time in hiding, and shorten the list of resources they can take with them.
Extending	**Add Extreme Weather:** Tell the students that, given the current pattern of extreme weather affecting the United States (possibly driven by climate change), they must plan to deal with extreme weather events (for example, higher tides, decreased rainfall, or increased snowfall) as part of their exercise. **Individual Versus Group?** Would it be easier or harder to do this activity as an individual, rather than as a group? Which needs in Maslow's hierarchy would be easier to meet as an individual? Which would be harder? What do you think the optimum size of a group would be if going into hiding for a year or more? Why do you think this?

ASSESSMENT NOTES
Because this is a completely open-ended activity, teachers should identify key expectations of students in their projects. Ideally, the students will work with the teacher to collaboratively develop a rubric for the final product.

Table 9.2. Data sources for real-time celestial sphere data

Activity	Website	URL	QR Code
Photoperiods	USNO *Complete Sun and Moon Data for One Day*	http://aa.usno.navy.mil/data/docs/RS_OneDay.php	
Solar Terminator	USNO *Day and Night Across the Earth*	http://aa.usno.navy.mil/data/docs/earthview.php	
	Timeanddate.com *Day and Night World Map*	http://timeanddate.com/worldclock/sunearth.html?iso=20161221T1044&=25	
Tonight's Sky	USNO *Topocentric Configuration of Major Solar System Bodies*	http://aa.usno.navy.mil/data/docs/ssconf.php	
	USNO *Rise/Set/Transit Times for Major Solar System Bodies and Bright Stars*	http://aa.usno.navy.mil/data/docs/mrst.php	
Hiding Out	USGS *WaterQualityWatch*	http://waterwatch.usgs.gov/wqwatch	
	NOAA National Weather Service	www.weather.gov	
	NOAA *Storm Events Database*	www.ncdc.noaa.gov/stormevents	

Table 9.2. (*continued*)

Activity	Website	URL	QR Code
Hiding Out (*continued*)	Weather Underground *Historical Weather*	*www.wunderground.com/history*	
	U.S. Department of Agriculture (USDA) *County Maps*	*www.nass.usda.gov/Charts_and_Maps/ Crops_County*	
	USDA *VegScape Vegetation Condition Explorer*	*https://nassgeodata.gmu.edu/VegScape*	
	NOAA *Tide Predictions*	*https://tidesandcurrents.noaa.gov/ tide_predictions.html*	
	FlightAware	*https://flightaware.com/live*	
	USNO *Complete Sun and Moon Data for One Day*	*http://aa.usno.navy.mil/data/docs/ RS_OneDay.php*	

Table 9.3. Other Sources for Celestial Sphere Data

Website	Address	QR Code
Timeanddate.com *Date and Time Calculator*	*www.timeanddate.com/date/timeadd.html*	
Lunaf	*http://lunaf.com/space/sky-map*	
Sky Marvels	*www.skymarvels.com/infopages/solarsysteminfo.htm*	
Earth and Moon Viewer	*https://fourmilab.ch/cgi-bin/Earth/action?opt=-p*	
Journey North "Mystery Class" project	*www.learner.org/jnorth/mclass*	
American Association of Variable Star Observers	*www.aavso.org*	
USNO *Phases of the Moon*	*http://aa.usno.navy.mil/data/docs/MoonPhase.php*	
The National Institutes of Health	*http://imagej.nih.gov/ij*	

CELESTIAL SPHERE

Table 9.3. (*continued*)

Website	Address	QR Code
LatLong	*www.latlong.net*	
NASA Space Science Data Coordinated Archive	*http://nssdc.gsfc.nasa.gov*	
NASA Human Space Flight Realtime Data	*http://spaceflight.nasa.gov/realdata*	
U.S. Naval Observatory (USNO)	*www.usno.navy.mil/USNO*	
USNO *Sun or Moon Altitude/Azimuth Table*	*http://aa.usno.navy.mil/data/docs/AltAz.php*	

PART 3

GOING
FURTHER

BEYOND THE DATA

Throughout this book we have mostly focused our investigations, whether using real-time and archived data, on two things: (1) using "stored" numeric data (that is, previously created variables) so that students sample already-available data sets to conduct their own research and answer their own questions from it, and (2) having students create their *own* variables and constructs from available information to repurpose it to answer new questions about new variables. Although we believe that doing this type of science investigation work develops students' science literacy—and given that secondary data analysis is a time-honored research method in science—these activities are still typical science activities in that students are collecting data, conducting data analysis, and constructing arguments from those activities, and are then writing conclusions about them using some form of science report.

However, the utility of science and its findings extend far beyond the areas in which scientists (and science students) work, and often extend into areas of interest to the public, where it can form and shape public policy. Given this, another science activity and skill we consider quite important is having students write about science findings and conclusions for readers who are not terribly scientifically literate on many issues—essentially, the general public. Even scientists themselves are now being encouraged to write about their research work for the general public, and many colleges and universities have developed science-communication programs and degrees to improve the communication of science research findings to nonspecialist audiences. So for us, an important aspect of science literacy, and one that we want to develop in our own students, is the ability to understand the findings of science and then to communicate that information to people with less of a science background through less-formalized communication strategies.

As teachers, we have also noted that students appreciate some variety in their writing tasks, so in this chapter we have included some activities that involve writing about the science data found using small devices (apps and/or websites) for different audiences and in different ways than for the previous activities. We would like to suggest that you consider using activities like these when you have an opportunity to, because research suggests that students write differently (and often better) when they are writing for an audience other than a teacher.

These sorts of nontraditional writing activities can take many forms. Students can use the information on the websites we have highlighted here to create posters and trifold

brochures, write a children's story (to teach someone much younger about the science behind an important issue), create a play, make a video for internet viewing, write an article for a newspaper, and so forth. This sort of activity also develops generic communication and literacy skills, so a science teacher might consider collaborating on an activity with another teacher (such as the art or language teacher)—an important consideration given that some schooling jurisdictions have a strong focus on math and literacy skills these days. What follows are a few ideas for using small devices to develop big ideas.

ATMOSPHERE

TEACHER NOTES: CHALLENGING THE SKEPTICS

Overview	Students will write an editorial to support an argument related to climate change.
Disciplinary Core Ideas	• Human impacts on Earth systems • Global climate change
Science and Engineering Practices	• Engaging in argument from evidence • Obtaining, evaluating, and communicating information
Crosscutting Concepts	• Energy and matter: Flows, cycles, and conservation • Stability and change
App and Device Sources	*Skeptical Science* app Platforms: iOS, Android
Student Instructions	In the app, browse one of the main categories of argument against climate change or one of the most-used arguments, and choose one that interests you. Summarize and compare "the "skeptic argument" (red), what "the science says" (green), and the additional information that supports the science (black). Write an editorial for a newspaper to support the science position as a rebuttal to an opinion column that took the skeptic position. Use scientific evidence to support your claims. Be sure to address the skeptic's concerns.

GEOSPHERE

TEACHER NOTES: EARTHQUAKE!

Overview	Students will create an earthquake safety brochure for the Federal Emergency Management Agency (FEMA).
Disciplinary Core Ideas	• Plate tectonics and large-scale system interactions • Natural hazards
Science and Engineering Practices	• Constructing explanations and designing solutions • Obtaining, evaluating, and communicating information
Crosscutting Concepts	• Energy and matter: Flows, cycles, and conservation • Stability and change
App and Device Sources	*American Red Cross Earthquake* app Platforms: iOS, Android
Student Instructions	For this assignment, imagine that you work for FEMA. Your job is to create a trifold brochure to give to people who live near a tectonic fault to warn them of the dangers of earthquakes. Write the information in your own words and include these topics: 1. What causes earthquakes and where they are likely to occur 2. Earthquake magnitude (energy) and how it is measured 3. Earthquake intensity (effect) and how it is measured 4. Hazards 5. Precautions and safety Be creative! Have fun!

HYDROSPHERE

TEACHER NOTES: HURRICANE "ME" IN THE NEWS

Overview	Students will write a newspaper article about an approaching hurricane.
Disciplinary Core Ideas	• Weather and climate • Natural hazards
Science and Engineering Practices	• Constructing explanations and designing solutions • Obtaining, evaluating, and communicating information
Crosscutting Concepts	• Cause and effect: Mechanism and explanation • Energy and matter: Flows, cycles, and conservation
App and Device Sources	*American Red Cross Hurricane* app Platforms: iOS, Android
Student Instructions	A hurricane with your name is threatening the U.S. Gulf Coast! You are a weather reporter for a local newspaper. Write an article for the paper describing this hurricane and what precautions residents in threatened areas should take. Be sure to explain how hurricanes form and how they are rated, what to worry about and what to do, and what recent hurricane activity there has been for your location on the Gulf Coast. When writing for a newspaper, an "inverted pyramid" approach is often used. Research what this approach is to make your article more authentic!

BEYOND THE DATA

HYDROSPHERE

TEACHER NOTES: NATIONAL PARK TRAVEL GUIDES

Overview	Students will create a travel brochure for a national park.
Disciplinary Core Ideas	• Earth materials and systems • Biogeology
Science and Engineering Practices	• Planning and carrying out investigations • Obtaining, evaluating, and communicating information
Crosscutting Concepts	• System and system models • Energy and matter: Flows, cycles, and conservation
App and Device Sources	*REI National Park Guide and Maps* app (for national parks information) Platforms: iOS, Android
	Weather History Explorer app (for climate data) Platforms: iOS, Android
Student Instructions	Create a travel brochure for one national park. Use information from the *REI National Park Guide and Maps* and *Weather History Explorer* apps, as well as from a mapping app or software program (for example, Google Maps) and other resources. In your brochure, include data about the park's climate, landforms, biome, rivers, location, history, native plants and animals, and things to do and see on a visit there.

ATMOSPHERE

TEACHER NOTES: STRATOSPHERIC OZONE

Overview	Students will summarize current stratospheric ozone levels.
Disciplinary Core Ideas	• Earth materials and systems • Human impacts on Earth systems
Science and Engineering Practices	• Developing and using models • Obtaining, evaluating, and communicating information
Crosscutting Concepts	• Patterns • System and system models
App and Device Sources	*NASA EarthNow* app Platforms: iOS, Android
Student Instructions	In the National Aeronautics and Space Administration's *NASA EarthNow* app, select "Vital Signs" and then "Ozone" to get the latest data in the app. Notice that data are shown in color ranges, with greenish-blue being the color for a mean (average) of 300 dobson units (DU) of ozone. You must interpret the data using the color scale. 1. What is the ozone level currently like over your region of the country? What is the approximate reading? 2. Where in the world are the highest ozone levels? What is the reading? 3. Where in the world are the lowest ozone levels? What is the reading? 4. Which satellite provides the ozone data? Go to the "Details" function and at the bottom of the screen, select "Animated Data." 5. Describe the changes you see in the ozone layer over the past week. 6. Explore one other data set. Write a summary of the data set you explored and what you discovered in the data provided.

CHAPTER 10

BIOSPHERE

TEACHER NOTES: WE ARE THE WORLD

Overview	Students will create an advertisement for a world hunger awareness program.
Disciplinary Core Ideas	• Biogeology • Natural resources
Science and Engineering Practices	• Asking questions and defining problems • Obtaining, evaluating, and communicating information
Crosscutting Concepts	• System and system models • Energy and matter: Flows, cycles, and conservation
App and Device Sources	*FAO NOW* app Platforms: iOS, Android
Student Instructions	This app includes events and success stories from the Food and Agriculture Organization (FAO) of the United Nations 1. Use the app to learn about and summarize three recent events in world hunger. Choose one story from "News," one from "In Action," and one from "Zero Hunger." Write a summary for each. 2. Use what you learn to create a hypothetical charity to raise money and awareness for world hunger. You can choose to create a poster, or a short video or a webpage, to advertise and promote your new organization. Include examples from the app.

11

REAL-TIME CITIZEN SCIENCE

The use of bring-your-own-technology (BYOT) is not limited to independent investigations using real-time data. There are a number of ways in which students can participate in the language and culture of science by collecting and sharing real-time data within a larger scientific community. Citizen science projects offer opportunities to participate and collaborate in real science experiences and add to ongoing investigations. According to Silvertown (2009, p. 467), "A citizen scientist is a volunteer who collects and/or processes data as part of a scientific enquiry". Citizen science projects are investigations designed by professional scientists that provide a role for amateur scientists. They are designed to provide educational benefits for the public as well as make scientific progress toward a project's goals. These projects are different from the work being done exclusively by scientists in that they are open to the public collection of data. Citizen science projects are an "ideal opportunity for science novices to become familiar with the process and culture of science and even to become engaged participants in the scientific enterprise" (Fenichel and Schweingruber 2010). Citizen science projects are not new. China has more than 1,200 years of cherry blossom data and more than 3,500 years of data on locust outbreaks. A more-modern example of an ongoing citizen science project is the Christmas Bird Count, an ongoing project that has been sponsored by the National Audubon Society (*www.audubon.org*) every year since 1900 (Silvertown 2009). Not only do these projects encourage public participation in data collection, but their records are freely available online.

Involvement in citizen science projects can have lasting effects on people who take part in them. Participating in citizen science projects can also lead to increased interest in science and changes in identity as volunteers begin to see themselves as part of a larger scientific community (Fenichel and Schweingruber 2010), which is certainly true from the authors' perspectives. In the early 2000s, Donna participated in a summer workshop that included making observations for the American Association of Variable Star Observers (AAVSO) (*www.aavso.org*). This organization was established in 1911, and for more than a century has collected observations from amateur astronomers around the world to monitor variable stars. Variable stars change magnitude and can tell us much about stellar evolution and our universe. Some types of variable stars have changes in magnitude that are very quick and can be observed in a single evening, whereas others have cycles that are decades long. Over the course of a single summer workshop, Donna collected data in an investigation that not only deepened her understanding of both science content and how science works, but also cultivated in her a life-long love of astronomy. Involvement in citizen science projects has lasting impact.

The internet has increased participation in citizen science projects because it now is easier than ever for scientists to reach out to the public and promote participation. This outreach has been a positive feedback loop, with the increased participation by the public then helping scientists to realize the general public is a wonderful, free resource for data collection. Because of this, scientists are creating even more opportunities for citizen science involvement in their work. Massive data sets have been collected, much larger than any scientist could collect alone, and within a geographically broader area (Miller-Rushing et al. 2012). Other factors that have led to the increased number of opportunities to participate in citizen science projects include the emphasis on public outreach in all National Science Foundation (NSF)–funded grants (Silverton 2009).

Educators who want to use citizen science projects in their classrooms "can engage learners in science while immersing them in science content and scientific practices" (Nugent et al. 2015, p. 35), and will find a multitude of projects to choose from for any content area. There are five general characteristics of a good citizen science project to look for (Silvertown 2009) in assessing projects:

1. A way to validate data: It is important that a scientist who wants to use data collected by the public can determine that the data are valid. Once data are entered into a project, they should be verifiable by a scientist within the project. This can happen in a number of ways. Images and geotags can be collected with data, and observations can be made using smartphones. Another means is to have multiple volunteers that analyze the same data; for example, identifying features on images.

2. Having standardized and well-designed methods: For data to be valid, all participants collecting and sharing those data should understand the protocols. Some projects include a training component. For example, the AAVSO has a training manual. Clemson University's *Firefly* app has a tutorial to help novices learn what data to collect and how to collect it.

3. Explicit assumptions: Any assumptions included in the investigation must be clearly communicated because the scientist usually will not be available to answer questions. A detailed FAQ (frequently asked questions) document or detailed "About" section is usually provided on project-related websites and apps.

4. Tentative hypothesis to guide data collection: Although not essential for a successful citizen project, having a tentative hypothesis is helpful for those collecting data to see the big picture.

5. Feedback to volunteers who collect data: Feedback can come in many different forms. In some projects, such as Project Noah (*www.projectnoah.org*), participants

can participate in "missions" and earn "patches" that show they have collected certain types of data. Other projects include opportunities to be included in publications when discoveries are made. Donna knows at least one amateur astronomer who published findings in a professional journal from participation in the AAVSO project.

Citizen science projects do not typically include all five characteristics, but those that include at least some of these features are desirable.

ESTABLISHED CITIZEN SCIENCE PROJECTS

Table 11.1 (p. 246) lists a variety of websites for citizen science projects. One of the most well-known citizen science projects in Earth science is the GLOBE project (Global Learning and Observations to Benefit the Environment, *www.globe.gov*). This government-sponsored program has been around since 1995 and is managed by NASA. It is designed for educators, and teachers must be trained at a workshop before their classes can participate. This project sets a high standard for protocols and standardization of data-collection methods, but provides teachers with in-depth lessons for implementation of their project in the classroom. Participating teachers can collect data for weather, soil, water quality, and various ecosystem indicators, such as land cover and mosquito-larvae counts. The training requirement for teachers assures that standard protocols are used in data collection. Because attending a face-to-face workshop can be inconvenient, some training modules are posted online. These are interactive video components that have required activities built in, to ensure thoroughness while teachers work through the modules. The emphases on training and protocols are important, because scientists use the data collected by teachers and students in real scientific investigations. Scientists are accessible to the students and teachers participating in the program, and they often collaborate with investigations. The GLOBE website has a responsive design and works smoothly on smartphones and tablets.

Another long-running citizen science program is Journey North (*www.learner.org/jnorth*), which is sponsored by Annenberg Learner and has been ongoing since 1997. This project involves students of all ages in tracking and reporting different indicators of seasonal changes. Journey North has developed an app to make reporting observations easy (Figure 11.1, p. 242). They are kid-friendly and provide information about the species included in their annual migration projects and other educational materials. Donna has experience with this program and been a fan since its early days. Projects include tracking migrations of hummingbirds, monarch butterflies, and American robins, as well as other seasonal indicators, such as tulip blooming and the first run of maple syrup. One of Donna's favorite projects is the Mystery Class activity, because of its interdisciplinary nature. This project runs each spring and is designed as a classroom activity in which students analyze multiple types of data, learn to calculate photoperiods, and use clues to identify 10 different mystery cities at different latitudes. The project is centered around the vernal equinox, so students see how

Figure 11.1.
Journey North app screenshot

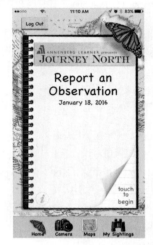

Source: Annenberg Learner. *www.learner.org.* Used with permission.

photoperiods vary above and below the equator. Students collect and analyze data on how the photoperiod changes at their own location as seasons change, and learn map and globe skills in a multicultural activity while using clues to identify 10 specific locations around the world. Donna has found that this activity is engaging and appropriate for students of all ages, and has used some variation of the project with elementary, middle school, and high school students over the past two decades. Regardless of which project you collect data for, the data collected as part of all projects are shared on the website and available to you. Collecting data on seasonal changes in this way has become more popular with the increasing importance of climate change in science.

The JASON Project (*www.jason.org*) is another long-running citizen science program that has been around for decades. Established in 1989 by Dr. Robert Ballard as an outgrowth of his Titanic expedition, this program is sponsored by National Geographic and now a fully developed curriculum project. Sponsorship of citizen science activities is just part of their portfolio. Real-time data projects include Budburst, which monitors seasonal changes, and the World Water Monitoring Challenge, in which students monitor water quality and report findings to a world-wide database.

CITIZEN SCIENCE PROJECT COLLECTIONS

One of the most well-known online forums for authentic, citizen science research is Zooniverse (*www.zooniverse.org*), and one of its longest-running projects is Galaxy Zoo, in which the public has helped classify images of galaxies since 2007. Although there are few opportunities for students to collect real-time data in these projects, participants are involved in processing visual data collected by scientists in authentic investigations. These projects are exciting in that scientific discoveries are continuously being made thanks to the help of the public. More than four dozen professional papers have been published from the efforts of this project. Other projects in the Zooniverse include identification of bat calls, studies of chimpanzee behavior, and identification of plankton.

Another great collection of citizen science projects can be found at SciStarter (*http://scistarter.com*), which began in 2010 and links interested citizen scientists to more than 1,100 projects in all fields of science (Figure 11.2). Funding for this project comes from the NSF and other public and private supporters. What Donna likes best about SciStarter is the ability to search for projects by content area or location of data collection (for example, home, car, or beach.). It also has resources online to help teachers select the right projects for their students and identify which projects include curriculum materials. The SciStarter database of projects is shared with the Public Broadcasting Service (see *pbs.org*) (PBS), the

National Science Teachers Association (NSTA), *Discover Magazine,* and many other broadcasters and publishers of science content. They are the ultimate resource for finding and locating projects to use in the classroom.

The Lost Ladybug Project (*www.lostladybug.org*) is one project to which SciStarter links (Figure 11.3). This citizen science project asks participants to identify and share images of ladybugs, which are used to track native and non-native species. The website provides educational materials that are suited to elementary-age students. The activities include lesson plans, handouts, reading lists, and other materials perfect for development of an integrated teaching unit. Participants in the project take geotagged photographs of ladybugs, add comments about the local habitat, and upload them to the project. Submissions are confirmed with the observer by email. An app can be downloaded, allowing for mobile participation, or data can be submitted directly from the app. Students can explore the current geographic range of sightings for different types of ladybugs, add to those data, and compare them to the 1985 geographic range for each species. This project is ideal for even the youngest citizen scientists!

The quantity of citizen science projects available for participation is too great to even begin listing here, and that landscape is always changing. Some projects are phasing out as goals are reached, and others are starting up each day, as scientists increasingly recognize the potential of public participation in real-time data collection. The chances are very good that whatever topic your class is studying, there is an opportunity for the students to participate in authentic science investigations through any number of projects. Alternatively, you could design your own projects for online or smartphone data collection outside the classroom or, through online resources, you can participate in other real-time citizen science projects designed by other teachers.

Figure 11.2. *SciStarter* **website screenshot**

Source: SciStarter. *http://scistarter.com.* Used with permission.

Figure 11.3. Lost Ladybug Project app screenshot

Source: Lost Ladybug Project. *www. lostladybug.org.* Used with permission.

BUILDING YOUR OWN PROJECT

As you continue collecting your own real-time data, you might decide you would like students to be able to collect and report data using their own devices. You might want to limit these data to what your students collect, or possibly decide to collaborate in real-time investigations with other classes. Such collaborations can provide broader results and can be used to compare the effects of phenomena at different locations. A number of online resources make it possible to set up and share data-collection programs easily. These citizen science applications are still fairly new, having been around only a few years. The websites might not be as stable as those of established projects shared in the Citizen Science Project Collections section, and might still need fine tuning to make them easier for students in classrooms to use. We expect to see more of these opportunities develop in the coming years, with these and other sites finding a stable niche in the online citizen science community.

CitSci (*www.citsci.org*) is one such resource that not only hosts hundreds of existing citizen science projects, but also allows teachers to create their own. Projects can be accessed on the web or through the *CitSci* app. This program was developed at Colorado State University by their Natural Resources Ecology Lab, with funding from the NSF. Although we found that some projects on their site lack the information needed for full participation, CitSci would be a viable option for the classroom teacher who wants to set up a project for students and collaborate with others.

A similar resource is Aecern (*www.aecern.com*), whose partners include the Woods Hole Oceanographic Institute, the Kaput Center at the University of Massachusetts, and Sana health care. Their website is exciting in that many of the projects designed either become stand-alone apps or are integrated into existing general apps for students to collect and report specific data. Teachers can choose existing projects to assign or create their own for student data collection. To start using this website, you must first set up a classroom account and either choose an existing project or create a new one. As the teacher, you add the students to your account and specify the data you want students to collect. All members of the class share the same account. The teacher must use a personal identification number when logging on to access the teacher section of the account. Once a project has been assigned, students can collect and submit their data. Teachers then have access to those data through the website.

Small World Data (*http://smallworlddata.com*) is a relatively new site developed by Donna's software-engineer husband for her to create authentic projects to use with her students. We can guarantee it will be around until she retires! This responsive-design website is ideal for using within a web browser or as a web-based app (Figure 11.4). It was built for teachers to develop projects for students to collect and share data in real time. Teachers create an account and set up new projects or collaborate with existing ones, and can upload complete lesson plans to share with colleagues.

In Small World Data, once a project has been assigned, a QR Code can be generated and posted for students or printed in their lesson plans. Students can scan the QR Code to enter data on their device or log into the website to report their data. Data can be geo-tagged and/or have images added. Teachers and students then can download a spreadsheet containing the data collected in the investigation to use for analysis. This website was developed with collaboration in mind so that teachers can share data synchronously or asynchronously with each other, regardless of location.

Such build-your-own-project websites are fairly new on the citizen science scene, but demonstrate a trend toward authentic engagement in collaborative science investigations. Most of their developers are genuinely interested in facilitating meaning scientific investigations for students and teachers, and are likely to be helpful when teachers reach out for help. Their websites and apps are also more likely to evolve over the coming years as demand for these types of projects increases.

As authors of a book that refers to websites and apps, we offer this reminder that websites appear and disappear every day, and this could happen with some we have mentioned. Should this occur, please remember that new opportunities will emerge in their place and can often be found with a simple internet search.

Whether you decide to involve your students in real-time investigations using data collected by another source or have them collect their own data, we feel that you and your students will find these authentic learning tasks meaningful and become more engaged in exploring Earth and environmental science. In addition, we hope that as a teacher, you will also find other new and exciting real-time data resources to use in your classroom.

Figure 11.4. *Small World Data iOS app screenshot*

Welcome to the World of Citizen Science Data!

STUDENTS AND DATA COLLECTORS:

Collect data and contribute to data sets! Cooperate with others to build useful data, find averages and deviations, and identify patterns and trends!

TEACHERS AND SCIENTISTS

Collaborate with your fellow teachers and scientists everywhere to design data layouts, create and share data sets, teach the scientific method, and build our base of knowledge!

Public Data Sets

Source: Small World Data. *http://smallworlddata.com.*

Table 11.1. Websites for citizen science

Citizen Science Source	URL	QR Code
CitSci	*www.citsci.org*	
Globe Project	*www.globe.gov*	
JASON Project	*www.jason.org*	
Journey North	*www.learner.org/jnorth*	
SciStarter	*http://scistarter.com*	
Small World Data	*http://smallworlddata.com*	
Zooniverse	*www.zooniverse.org*	

REFERENCES

Annenberg Learner. 2012. *Journey North* app. *www.learner.org*.

Fenichel, M., and H. A. Schweingruber. 2010. *Surrounded by science: Learning science in informal environments*. Washington, DC: National Academies Press.

Lost Ladybug Project. 2016. *Lost Ladybug Project* app. *www.lostladybug.org*.

Miller-Rushing, A., R. Primack, and R. Bonney. 2012. The history of public participation in ecological research. *Frontiers in Ecology and the Environment* 10 (6): 285–290.

Nugent, J., L. Cook, M. Bell, and W. Smith. 2015. 21st-century citizen science. *The Science Teacher* 82 (8): 34–38.

SciStarter. 2016. SciStarter. *http://scistarter.com*.

Silvertown, J. 2009. A new dawn for citizen science. *Trends in Ecology and Evolution* 24 (9): 467–471.

Small World Data LLC. 2016. *Small World Data* app. *http://smallworlddata.com*.

ACTIVITY REFERENCES

CHAPTER 5

Climate.gov. *www.climate.gov*

FlightAware. 2016. *https://flightaware.com/live.*

GISTEMP Team. GISS Surface Temperature Analysis (GISTEMP). NASA Goddard Institute for Space Studies. *http://data.giss.nasa.gov/gistemp.*

National Weather Service. *http://forecast.weather.gov/MapClick.php?lat=41.57263&lon=-93.61571&unit =0&lg=english&FcstType=graphical.*

CHAPTER 6

Central Intelligence Agency. CIA *World Factbook. https://cia.gov/library/publications/resources/the-world-factbook.*

U.S. Department of Agriculture. *National Drought Monitor. http://droughtmonitor.unl.edu/ MapsAndData/DataTables.aspx.*

CHAPTER 7

Barouline, S. 2016. *Volcanoes: Map, alerts, earthquakes and ash clouds app.*

Environmental Protection Agency. *Radon. www.epa.gov/radon/find-information-about-local-radon-zones-and-radon-programs.*

Rice University. Plate motion calculator widget. *http://tectonics.rice.edu/hs3.html.*

U.S. Geological Survey. *Plate tectonic map. http://pubs.usgs.gov/gip/dynamic/slabs.html.*

U.S. Geological Survey. *Volcano Hazards Program U.S. Volcanoes and Current Activity Alerts. http:// volcanoes.usgs.gov/index.html.*

CHAPTER 8

Engineering Goodness LLC. 2016. *NOAA Buoy Data* app. Quincy, MA. *http://noaabuoydata.com.*

National Oceanic and Atmospheric Administration. *Tides and currents tide predictions. https:// tidesandcurrents.noaa.gov/tide_predictions.html.*

National Snow and Ice Data Center. 2016. *Arctic sea ice news and analysis. https://nsidc.org/ arcticseaicenews.*

Savchenko, V. 2014. *Weather History Explorer* app. Sofia, Bulgaria.

U.S. Geological Survey. *WaterQualityWatch. http://waterwatch.usgs.gov/wqwatch.*

CHAPTER 9

Colarusso, D. *Bureaucrats and Mathemagicians: Data Science and Public Defenders. www.davidcolarusso.com/astro.*

Powell, M. J. 2007. *Naked Eye Planets. www.nakedeyeplanets.com/star-chart-lab-printer-friendly.png.*

U.S. Naval Observatory. USNO *Complete Sun and Moon Data for One Day. http://aa.usno.navy.mil/data/docs/RS_OneDay.php.*

U.S. Naval Observatory. USNO *Day and Night Across the Earth. http://aa.usno.navy.mil/data/docs/earthview.php.*

U.S. Naval Observatory. USNO *Topocentric Configuration of Major Solar System Bodies. http://aa.usno.navy.mil/data/docs/ssconf.php.*

INDEX

Page numbers in **boldface** type refer to tables or figures.